The Other Side of Love

By

Carole Lenzy Daniel (Marlowe)

This book is a work of fiction. Places, events, and situations in this story are purely fictional. Any resemblance to actual persons, living or dead, is coincidental.

ISBN: 1-4033-9167-X (e-book)
ISBN: 1-4033-9168-8 (Paperback)

This book is printed on acid free paper.

1stBooks - rev. 05/23/03

Dedication

For Mom

Thanks to Lynda

Author's Notes

Violence against women affects everyone. The statistics are alarming:

. One out of every three women worldwide is affected by violence.

. One out of every four women have been a victim of sexual assault.

. Nearly two million women are physically assaulted, some murdered, by their male partners every year.

Women and men need to stand together and speak out to stop The Violence. Together, we can make a difference. Women from all backgrounds, ethnicity's and sexual orientations have a voice. Please, let it be heard!

Marlowe-

Table of Contents

About the Book

Absolutely, an erotic thriller

and mysterious love story!

Prologue

O'Hare International Airport Chicago - 2002

"May I have your attention please! United Airlines flight number 237 from O'Hare International in Chicago to JFK has been delayed approximately thirty minutes due to severe weather. We apologize for this inconvenience."

"Oh well, I guess I'll go get those souvenirs I promised the boys. Mom, since our flight has been delayed will you be alright here for say fifteen minutes or so?"

"Yes. You go on. I'll be just fine."

Chapter One

Robinson High – Three Years Earlier

It was late August. The air smelled of dust blown gently by a soft breeze, which cooled the hot afternoons. School had started up again. The usual first week or so of excitement rang high in the Student's voices as they readily passed between classes after nearly three months vacation.

Carole Lenzy Daniel (Marlowe)

There was something beautiful about this year. After so many years of ups and downs and confusion during the first month or so of school, this year would be different. It even, at times, gave me qualms of apprehension for I feared it would explode with a terrible mishap any day. Something for which I kept myself constantly prepared. Of course there were few misunderstandings of little capacity, which were quickly taken care of by my two assistants. For that, I was left quite alone a great deal of the time. Time...

time to myself in my office to relax, read or whatever. Even meetings normally held elsewhere were held in my office from time to time. The School Superintendent came to me or called when there was something of importance to be brought to my attention. I suppose they were all quite aware of my slight heart attack the previous year and my determination to continue being Head Principal at Robinson High, as I had been for

Carole Lenzy Daniel (Marlowe)

nearly twenty-five years, in spite of it.

On occasions there were fresh flowers brought in by my secretary from the staff to remind me that I had not been forgotten. After my morning announcements, I made very few appearances in the main office.

One morning, after scanning the Tribune and pushing aside the unneeded coffee I was about to indulge myself into the necessary daily reading materials when my door opened and

Mrs. Bartlett stood looking flush. "What is it?" I asked calmly.

"Excuse me ma'am, there is a gentleman in the main office demanding to see Miss Greene. Something about her referring that his son be transferred out of Chorus."

"Miss Greene? Oh yes, the new music teacher sent over from Eastern. She's supposed to be one of the best. Has she not reported in?"

"Not yet." She answered still looking flushed. "He seems very upset. I offered

5

him coffee and told him that Miss Greene would probably be in shortly."

"Was he accepting?"

"Not at all, he wants to see you immediately. Shall I show him in?"

"By all means, oh and Mrs. Bartlett when Miss Greene arrives ask her to come in also."

"Sure thing Mrs. Whittington."

I sat pondering over how I would calm the situation if needed. I rose to stare out of the only window behind my desk at the students now beginning to circulate in bunches on the school grounds. I also noticed my reflection in the mirror like window. My golden, grayish hair, frosted, and blue eyes amidst a still childlike face, in spite of being nearly fifty-five, was radiant. Thank God I still had somewhat of a figure and could dress in very fine, expensive attire.

The door opened again and Mrs. Bartlett appeared followed by a small, brown-skinned man with hoyden features. She introduced him as Mr.

Carole Lenzy Daniel (Marlowe)

Prandue then politely excused herself to her duties. I introduced myself in a rather lacuna manner while making a study of him. He had calmed himself somewhat and seemed eager to speak on the matter.

"Mrs. Whittington I did not come to make any trouble for you or that new lady music teacher." He glared distastefully. "I have a great deal of respect for this school and the people who represent the entire educational system within the district. But my boy...

Joey, music and singing are the only things he has always seemed to truly enjoy. He has always made excellent grades in music class. I...we just want to see our son doing something he enjoys and making something of himself rather than end up on the street like other children whose talent was wasted because some small incident was not properly looked into."

The door opened once more and I readily motioned for Miss Greene to come in. She quietly pulled out a chair

Carole Lenzy Daniel (Marlowe)

opposite Mr. Prandue. He continued as though Miss Greene's entrance went unnoticed by him.

"You do understand that I am merely a parent who is concerned about his child's better interest." He was pleading not taking his eyes from me to meet those of Miss Greene's whose were totally fixed on him.

"Joey, how does Joey feel about all of this?" I asked. "A...well...he has never had a problem with music..."

"Mr. Prandue my name is Angela Greene and I am Joey's music teacher." Miss Greene interrupted. "There seems to be some sort of misunderstanding. Might I entrust the fact that I requested Joey be transferred from my music class because Joey himself asked to be. Joey is an excellent music student, one of my best. Sure he has his moments and has been found quite guilty of arousing the class in a bit of mischievous however, he is very capable of showing promising achievement."

Carole Lenzy Daniel (Marlowe)

She eased back in her seat quietly. Her eyes displayed traces of pity for the gentleman sitting opposite her. The buzzer on the telephone broke the silence. I quickly lifted the receiver and whispered a soft, nearly futile, "yes" into it.

"Good Morning Ma'am," Mr. Stratton's harsh voice spoke, "Just buzzed to let you know that Malcombs will cover for Miss Greene, if need, this morning."

"Good deal, thanks for taking care of that."

"Sure thing."

I let the receiver fall into place lightly so as not to disturb the thoughts of either of them. I kept silent as I looked from one to the other for something, anything to be said. Mr. Prandue broke the silence.

"I was not aware that Joey wanted to be removed from the music course. It's so unlike him." He looked sad for a moment, then added, "But children do

13

grow up don't they? Before you know it they are making decisions for themselves and...well, I am sorry to have wasted your time. It seems that I should be taking this matter up with my son." Miss Greene continued dodging his eyes. Slowly he rose and extended his hand. "It's nice to have met you." Miss Greene accepted his hand and smiled. "Mrs. Whittington," he extended his hand a second time. I grasped it and commented on his being the kind of concerned parent we needed more of in our community. He slowly made his way to the door, bade us good-bye, then disappeared. Miss Greene sat staring with her hands clasped over her mouth. I slowly walked around my chair to stare, once again, out of the small window above it.

"He's a good kid."

"Who?"

"Joey Prandue. He's a good kid but he is lost."

"Lost!" I questioned grasping the back of my chair.

15

"Yes, lost!" She stammered.

"You yourself indicated that the boy was a trouble maker."

"Not necessarily a trouble maker, Mrs. Whittington, but a kid who is torn between his future and his peers." Her large brown eyes studied me.

"For that reason he has asked to be placed in another class? Why not place him into music class another period by rearranging his entire schedule?"

"No. I'm afraid that won't do either. I don't think Joey wants music in his life at all right now." She scratched her head; "Possibly it is more of a rebellious act against what Mom and Dad want for him rather than his loss of interest."

"You've sized him up quite well."

"Not really. It's only a matter of being able to really communicate with my students allowing them the freedom of speech when it comes to their true feelings."

"I agree." I replied. "I would be the first to acknowledge that there must be communication... a likeness inside a classroom before any degree of learning takes place, especially with kids of this era."

"I'm afraid Mr. Prandue has more of a problem than he thinks now that little Joey isn't so little anymore." Rising she neatly pushed her chair back into its proper place. "Thank you Mrs. Whittington."

"What for?" I asked surprised at her affable tone.

"For... for just being here. For listening."

"Well you are most welcome and should any other problem arise please don't hesitate to bring it to my attention. That's what I am here for." She smiled, looking no older than a student herself, thanked me again and promised that she would not hesitate one moment.

After she had gone, I buzzed my secretary and asked that she hold all of my calls. "I have some very important papers to go over before this afternoon's meeting with the Superintendent." I

Carole Lenzy Daniel (Marlowe)
said. I put down the receiver then stared, for a moment, at the stack of papers.

* * *

So the days at Robinson High passed pleasantly. Somehow the world felt cozy which made each day comfortable, as they grew shorter and cooler near the end of October. The Students were now quite settled into the school year. They looked forward to things such as PTA meetings, football games, pep assemblies and a drama put on by the school drama club, about Halloween, which was run during class time sixth period for all that had purchased tickets.

The sophomore music students under the direction of Miss Angela Greene one afternoon performed Songs to the musical OLIVER. It was such a success that my assistants and I were considering running it for the parents during back to school night. We did and it was a smash! The morning after there was a column in the Tribune about the successful musical given by the sophomore chorus of Robinson High and how well Miss Angela Greene had supervised and conducted such a task.

It was half past noon before I cleared my desk and started on my way to visit Miss Greene, in laudatory, about the wonderful performance given and to give my personal congratulations on behalf of the school faculty. Not only because it was my position to do so but also because I had enjoyed the musical as whimsically as anyone.

She was alone in her classroom, eating her lunch, as I walked in and placed the Tribune on the desk before her. I begged her pardon for interrupting and asked if I might have a few moments to visit with her. She motioned for me to pull up one of the desks.

She was a beautifully, handsome young woman. Her hair was dark nearly black with shimmering dabs of light tent. Her skin was the color of just right toast and her brows razor thin, which curved perfectly around large

brown eyes with thick curly lashes. She

looked no older than a high school

student herself. She was tall and slim

wearing a burgundy sweater, which

softened her features into the beautiful

feminist she was. She raised her eyes

from the Tribune and stared at me.

"What are you doing?"

"Staring and admiring. You look so

pretty and so young." She blushed

making her look even younger. Half-

smiling she timidly dropped her eyes

back to the Tribune. I could tell hat she was not too acquainted with an older woman telling her how nice she was to look at.

"I would offer you some lunch but I only brought enough for one."

"Thank you but I have eaten."

"Do forgive me," she yawned, "I'm afraid that I am very tired after last night." She looked up at the clock. "Ah, only two and a half more hours."

Carole Lenzy Daniel (Marlowe)

"Have you seen the write up in the Tribune? There is quite a nice bit in it about you."

"No, as a matter of fact I haven't. I hardly read the newspaper because of all of the violence it contains." She talked a while about what she believed in. Her religion and why she believed in it. Suddenly she was quiet, stared at me then commented, "You're agreeing with me."

"Does it surprise you?"

"Yes, Mrs. Whittington it does." She leaned forward with both elbows on the desk. "Do you read the Bible often?"

"I read a great deal of everything. I've studied all types of religion and have assembled with various ethnicities of people. I can tell that you are most certainly a person who cares very deeply for your music."

"It means everything to me. It is truly all I've ever desired to do, to write and perform before an audience that has

Carole Lenzy Daniel (Marlowe) appreciation for culturally diverse music."

"Then why don't you? You certainly have the qualifications needed."

"Oh... it's far more to it than that." She smiled showing off white straight teeth amidst her brown skin. "It's not like, boom, overnight you are a success. It is more hard work and constant preparation."

"And you can't handle that?"

"There are or were other obligations."

"Were?"

"Yes, I was married and unfortunately to someone who did not care about any musical talent of mine. He would never even admit that I had any talent. He wanted someone to be the mother of his children and remain in the shadows. I guess we were both too selfish. I just wasn't cut out to live that sort of sheltered life. I was never happy with him."

"It's hard to imagine you as a homemaker, I mean with all of your talent." I said studying her.

Carole Lenzy Daniel (Marlowe)
"I was not married very long, two years at most.

The distant chatter of the students now filled the hallways. I had been listening so intently that I had not heard the noon bell. I begged her pardon for staying as long as I had and asked if she would forgive me for taking her into such deep conversation. She smiled pleasantly and said that she had enjoyed every moment of it.

"Its not every day one meets someone that they can speak so openly with." She rose and handed me the Tribune. "As a matter of fact, I don't think I've ever engaged so deeply in conversation with anyone." The students came in noisily.

"We'll have to talk again soon." I said as I made my way to the door. As I turned to leave the classroom I felt her hand grasp my arm. When I faced her she whispered her breath warm against my ear; "I never enjoyed how he made love to me either."

"Who?"

"My husband."

"Attention please. United Airlines flight 237 to New York is now boarding at gate 13. Please have your tickets ready as you enter the boarding ramp. Thank you."

"Hello ma'am, will you be in need of assistance boarding the plane?" The attendant's smile was bright and cheerful.

"Thank you but no," I said smiling back, "My daughter is accompanying me."

"Mom, our flight is boarding." Jessica shouted approaching us. "Yes it is." I answered positioning my wheel chair so that she could grasp the handles.

"If you need anything at all please let us know." The attendant smiled once again and made a path for my chair to board quickly so that I could be helped into my seat.

"Good morning ladies and gentleman. We've reached our cruising altitude of approximately thirty-five thousand feet and we expect a smooth ride. I have turned off the seatbelt sign and you are free to move about the cabin." The pilot's deep voice echoed throughout the plane.

"Well now, after all of that I do need to go to the restroom. How about you Mom, do you need anything?" Jessica asked releasing her seatbelt and rising slowly.

"No thank you I am just fine. Perhaps I'll need to go in an hour or so."

I thought a great deal about her after that. I even found myself longing to be in her company. I promised myself that I would not go to her room for lunch anymore and that I would forget about this young woman in which I had grown so fond of in such a short time. Still, I would find myself on the stairway leading to her room excited with anticipation of our conversations. The more we were together the more we wanted to be. She would stop in my

Carole Lenzy Daniel (Marlowe)

office an hour or so before school began

and we would sometimes spend nearly

two hours after school there. While

together we talked of everything from

her love life to reciting famous poetry.

We would even go so far as imitating

famous actresses in their most notable

roles, love story roles.

"You're in love with love." I would tell

her and one morning she surprised me

with a poem of how she viewed our

relationship.

She wrote:

If only I had met you a different time and place, a time when love was true love, when youth shown in your face. If only time had held you still, if God himself had willed, our love yours and mine to be one the whole world could see. If only dreams were dreamed to come true, then I would dream that I had you on a frosty, chilly snow fallen eve with intense, dramatic movements to please indeed a virtuous beauty it would be. If time itself could call you back or permit me advancement in years, then my fears would be no fears

and together would be our aging

years. If even now as it is we could say

the things in our hearts instead of

playing our roles and acting our parts.

Satan himself would come to see this

unusual love one he has permitted

none to be until this time a time too

late when true love has been hidden

within the shadows of hate. If only we

could hide ourselves from the master

above to enjoy this love would we still

make it to heaven? Oh, could we love be ever forgiven?

I was impressed and after that we started seeing each other. Regardless of my age when I was with Angie I was a child at heart.

Suddenly the days took on a faster pace, seemingly. Time was running away. If it had not been for that I do fear that my husband would have grown more suspicious about the weekends I spent out of town with Angie. It was not that I loved him any

Carole Lenzy Daniel (Marlowe)

less, I had only found a key to the door

which awakened a violently,

passionate love I never realized could

exist within me until now.

* * *

Greatly daring one evening we

visited the Assembly Center where the

opera MADAME BUTTERFLY was being

performed for one exclusive week. What

an evening! Angie had been correct in

her prediction of there being a great

crowd opening night. We were

fortunate in our casualness not to be

recognized in the darkness. As the final

tune was being played we made our

way to the car hand in hand. We heard

roaring cheers from the crowd as the

performers finished up the night.

It was midnight when we entered the

Hilton. After gentle caresses and tender

kisses I undressed as Angie poured each

of us a glass of champagne, afterwhich,

our kisses were soft and gentle. The feel

of Angie's body next to mine was that of

silk. I wanted her so deeply, so

passionately; I could feel the wetness

between my legs as I caressed her. The rhythm of our lovemaking soared. A grim smile of satisfaction came about her lips as she climaxed and I knew she was thinking of our first night together. The night we both came to realize was the beginning of a new and exciting relationship, New Years Eve.

As she opened her eyes I gently kissed her lips and drew her closer to me.

"I love you Angie." I said still caressing her. She looked up at me and smiled.

"A famous Greek poet once said that one is fortunate to find one true friend during the course of a lifetime."

"I'll agree with that," she said, "however I do believe that you and I have found that one true friend. But in order for us to love and really understand the meaning of true love we first had to become true friends."

"Is that a recapitulation of our relationship?"

"Of course, I do trust you to be the gallant knight I have always dreamed of." She giggled.

"Why do you laugh?"

"I was thinking that no one would ever imagine that my Knight would be a woman."

"And does that bother you?"

"Not at all. I don't think I could ever have found a more gorgeous one." With that she raised herself on one elbow and gently kissed my lips. "I love you

Ella. I'll never love anyone the way that

I love you. I've never felt this way about

anyone before." As she smiled down at

me, her black skin against my paleness,

I began gently kissing her breast and

drew her even closer to me.

"Then you will never leave me?" I

asked.

"Never!" We made passionate love

until dawn.

I would never forget those evenings

spent with Angie. Daring as they were

Carole Lenzy Daniel (Marlowe)
each moment held a special meaning.

We were in love. We were happy.

Chapter Two

Tragedy

I was sitting in my office, with Angie, one morning before school when she looked puzzled then said, "I'm leaving Robinson High Ella." My heart skipped a beat. Possibly I did not hear what I thought I had. She smiled apologetically. "Well, It couldn't go on forever, could it? My career, I'm finally getting that break I've desired for so long."

"Leaving? How could you? What about us?" I shouted.

She smiled at me but it was a sad smile. "You'll get over me. You still have your husband and family. This was something we both thought we needed in our lives and now it's over."

"Over! I love you Angie. You can't just up and leave, I can't let you go."

She shook her head, "Have to, my agent has informed me of an offer from a Symphony in New York."

"So you're moving to New York?" I cried feeling ridiculously childish.

"I've been waiting a long time for this and now it has finally come. Perhaps at the wrong time."

"When will you be leaving?"

She looked sad. "Sometime next month." I caught her up in my arms and drew her to me not caring if anyone walked in and caught us.

"I love you Ella." She said clinging helplessly to me. "I really love you."

"Don't go." I begged.

"I have to. I can't just pass up the greatest opportunity of my life. In case you haven't noticed I was not born blond with blue eyes. I wasn't even born on the right side of the tracks. Opportunities like this one do not come by people like me very often. You of all people should be able to understand that."

"I do understand and that's what hurts." I sighed.

"It's more to it than just becoming a name well known or a face everyone recognizes. It isn't even about signing autographs or being taken pictures of throughout the world. It is knowing within myself that I accomplished what I set out to do and being able to help others do the same."

I wanted to plead with her but I knew her mind was made up. I dared not try to imagine what it would be like once she was gone.

* * *

The news of her imminent departure was received in various ways. The Superintendent was proud to have employed a potential famous musician.

"I hope that one day she will return to us even if as a guest speaker." He commented.

Most of the other teachers and students were happy for her and felt that she did posses the talent to be successful within the music industry.

But I was the one desolate.

We planned all sorts of treats those final weeks, which seemed to only make it worse. There was no fun in sneaking out of town to watch a play or meeting after school in my office simply to be close to each other, if you knew it was the last time you were to be together.

We attended a Jazz concert ten miles outside of Chicago. Our last outing then she would be gone away forever. She too seemed sad. I supposed second-guessing her decision to depart from our blissful affair. We drove back in the car I had rented, neither of us caring very much whether we were recognized. I kissed her gently goodnight. and watched carefully until she was securely inside. I sat for a while in the car, uneasy because of her departure the next day. The moon was full and the clouds were heavy. It was two a.m. when I started the car and slowly pulled off.

I caught my breath for a sudden feeling of terror! Through my rear view mirror I saw a man coming out of Angie's apartment. It appeared to be the same man she had introduced to me as her agent when he came to the school to discuss her offer. Although his face was not clear I recognized his blond hair as it shimmered under the street lamp. What was he doing in Angie's apartment at this time of the morning? It could not possibly be to discuss business. I drew the car slowly back toward the curve and quietly turned off the engine. They hadn't noticed the movement of the car and it was to dark to see if anyone occupied it. He was talking with his back to the street. He reached into his pocket and handed a small packet inside the door to Angie, who accepted it willingly. He then bent and kissed her forehead and squeezed the hand, which held the packet. Her face was aglow with excitement. She yawned sleepily and shook her head as if answering no to some suggestion. The young man stood there until finally they both went back inside. I didn't know what to do. I sat still my mind was frozen. Was he her male lover? I imagined the two of them inside madly making love and all along she had planned to run away with him. I did so want to go to the door and confront them both. I may have done so. Instead I got out of the car and paced back and forth staring at the door for any type of movement. After an hour or so I got back into the car never taking my eyes off that door.

"What could they be doing?" I asked myself. I would confront Angie in the morning. I dozed a bit. It was sunrise when I was awakened by the sound of a car engine starting up. I straightened from my slump in the seat to watch him, the man who had spent the night in Angie's apartment, drive away. His hair looked somewhat tossed and sleep rode on the shadows of his face as he zoomed past. I felt a great relief though puzzled as to why he had spent over four hours with the woman I loved more than life itself. I had to go up and find out.

Sun streamed through the door as I stepped inside. How daylight changed everything like shutting away ugly shadows until darkness fell. I was to the point of mentioning the man to Angie but somehow thought the better of it. It was as though the night was gone forever and the only thing that mattered was she in my arms as I drew her close to me.

Carole Lenzy Daniel (Marlowe)

"Oh...Ella," she whispered, "how could you have known I needed you now?" We kissed violently with severe passion. Angie's lips gently made their way to my breast as her hands fought to get to my underwear. My fingers were deep inside her and all I remember was the nearly perfect rhythm of our love making.

* * *

That afternoon Angie left. I did not turn to watch her board the plane. Good-byes were too common and lovers such as ourselves did not need dramatic behavior to know that we did and always would belong to each other. As I exited the airport I wiped a fallen tear from my cheek. I felt as though fate had dealt me a bad hand. Why let me find true, blissful love, something that I never knew existed within me, then have it ripped away like a part of my body? I thought as I drove to return the rented car. At least I still had my family. Angie was right in mentioning that I could go back to

Carole Lenzy Daniel (Marlowe)

my little perfect, white, suburban-American world and live as if not any of this ever happened. It was, however, frightening to think what might have happened if word ever got out about our affair. We each might have lost our jobs.

My arrival at home was welcomed as always. My youngest, Jessica was home again and according to her, for good this time. With a colossal of suitcases and a son in each arm she relentlessly moved herself back into her old bedroom and the two boys into the guestroom. She explained to me privately that she had caught her husband in a relationship with another woman again but that this time she would be seeking a divorce.

"It was not easy to leave New York and the boys father but I simply could not let him continue to hurt us." She said proudly. "I just don't understand how someone can say they love you one day and not care if they rip you apart the next. He never really loved the boys or me. We were only something he reached out to have because he knew he could." I felt her heartache as I listened to her go on about how egotistical her husband had become. That was six months ago and I dare say that she was holding up pretty well. She even dated once.

I stopped, before going inside, to throw a long pass to my Grandson Billy who was in the front yard playing football with his brother Bradley. It was late afternoon and the chill of the evening began to set in. I brushed

through the living room and the group

of Alumni who met there every Sunday

to watch the NFL. I kissed my husband

gently and waved to the group.

After bathing long and luxuriously

in warm water, I found Winston at the

front door bidding his friends

goodnight. I put my arms around him

from behind. He embraced me as we

said our last farewell for the evening.

That night as we lie in bed Winston

mentioned that Reverend Morris asked

about me after services. He commented that he had not seen me within the past few weeks and was wondering how I was.

"I told him that you were busy with the closing semester at school, various meetings and so forth. He did mention that he would love for you to sponsor the Woman's Day program to be held the third Sunday next month if at all possible. I told him that I would make mention of it to you but you had to decide."

"When do I have to let him know?" I asked.

"The sooner the better in case he does have to find someone else it won't be last minute." He broke off slanting a guilty look. "Here I am talking up a storm and you've hardly had a chance to get a word in. I'm dying to know how your meeting went Ella."

"No different, as boring as ever, I'm tired and all I really want is to get some much needed sleep but first some good loving." I chuckled as I found

67

myself caught up in his arms. He kissed me gently on my forehead.

"I missed you as I always have when you must be away." He said gently. My hand reached for his penis. As I was guiding him inside I felt him sigh. I whispered how much he meant to me and then mentioned how we needed to take advantage of what time we did have left to share each other's love. "You know we are each getting older but somehow I just don't know where the time has gone." We began to get into the rhythm of our love making, As I neared my climax Winston cried out, I assumed from pleasure, as I came with moans of satisfaction. We lay still for some time his breathing heavy on my neck. After our lips were pressed firmly, he gently removed himself and rolled on his back. I reached once more for his penis and he cried out as if he were in some kind of pain. Dumbfounded, I quickly removed my hand and asked "Winston what on earth? I didn't squeeze too hard, did I?"

Carole Lenzy Daniel (Marlowe)

"No, no it's nothing like that."

"Then what is it?" You sounded as if you were experiencing some sort of pain." I asked concerned. He rolled over to face me and his face was, as pale as I had ever seen it.

"Ella I swore that I would never tell you. I never intended for you to find out but the pain... as you can see I can't control it anymore. Sooner or later you would figure it out any way."

"Figure what out? What is this all about?" I asked wondering if he had some knowledge of my relationship with Angie. "What sort of gossip have you been listening to?"

"Gossip?" he questioned with a raised brow. "What sort of gossip should I have been listening to?" He sat up in the bed. I, more baffled than before, sat up beside him. Winston, staring into open space, arms around his legs, knees in the air told me of the shocking news that was the cause of his behavior. He never looked at me once while he was talking. As I listened intently I felt a coldness spreading throughout my body. How could it be? How could God allow such a thing to happen to a person who was so caring and loved by everyone who knew him? When the last words had fallen from his lips we sat without speaking, without moving. I felt dead inside. I wish I had some answer, some magic word that would make all of this bad news nothing more than a practical joke. When I looked at Winston I knew there was no such word. Breaking the silence he spoke first.

"Ella?"

"Yes?"

He sighed as though he feared I had lost my power of speech. "Perhaps I should not have told you. Perhaps I should not have been told. It may have been easier to accept had it come suddenly, rather than all of the waiting. Just waiting for it to happen knowing there is no stopping what must happen." I nodded slowly not really meaning that I agreed or that I truly

Carole Lenzy Daniel (Marlowe) believed that there really was no more hope.

He ran his fingers through his hair, face contorted.

"Say something for god's sake." He cried. "Tell me that this can't be happening to me. That somehow I was given the wrong information and that my test results came back negative!"

"Damn it! Is it too much for me to ask for a miracle?" I threw myself in his arms. We both cried for a long time. Each muffled sob followed by another, stronger, louder sob. I wanted to tell him that we were each having a bad dream and by morning it would have all been forgotten. I could not.

It is of common human nature that when one has decided on a wrong course of action no matter how dishonest or criminal, the offender always has a justifiable reason. After the crushing news of my husband dying of cancer, no matter how hard I tried I, of all things, was still thinking of Angie. I somehow hoped that her

Carole Lenzy Daniel (Marlowe)

departure that afternoon was also a part of this bad dream. Before falling asleep I realized that I must get a grip and stare the bleak future blankly in the face.

* * *

I nearly over slept the following Monday morning. I had to rush out without breakfast to make it to my office before the eight a.m. bell. The students were clustered in the hallways, as usual, around my office as I made my way to the door with numerous.

"Good mornings".

Once inside I closed the door gently and slowly sat behind my desk. The morning Tribune was there as usual. However, my mind was not.

"It's impossible," I said aloud. "It can't be true. It must be some kind of sick joke!" I drank from the cup of coffee that was before me. What if it is true? What would be my alternative? I could go to Winston and confess everything to him about the relationship Angie and I had shared, before his death, then

Carole Lenzy Daniel (Marlowe)

after I could visit with my other

daughter in New York until I worked

out exactly what I would do. Of course,

I would have to resign as I had

already began formulating notes here

and there in my mind for my letter of

resignation. On the other hand, there

was this wild, preposterous plan which

my mind presented to me with all sorts

of notions, ideas and possibilities. This

is wrong, I kept telling myself. It is

ungodly even criminal. It should not

even be something I should be thinking

of at this time. In some ways though to contemplate it acted as a palliative. It took my mind off of the misery of death. Of course I could never do such a thing but it would be beautiful if it were accomplished. An hour slipped by. I was still thinking of it. I could go to New York, then London no one would ever think much else than that my desire to get away would be from grieving for my husband. The home that we had shared so many years in together would not be the best place for me, afterward. In fact

Carole Lenzy Daniel (Marlowe)

it would do me good to get away after

death had touched so close. The first

part would be easy. I could send in my

resignation the reason being that I

would want to spend my husband's last

months by his side. That was all so very

true. Immediately after the funeral I

could fly to New York. But then, what

about Jessica and the boys being left

alone in the house at such a sorrowful

time? I could not just leave them alone

like that. I thought a great deal about

it only I must leave it there and start thinking sensibly.

I spent a restless night. I kept dozing then dreaming of my going to New York and finding Angie. After running toward each other we gently embraced and she clung relentlessly to me. "We truly belong together," I said not loud enough for sleeping Winston to hear. I suppose I was awake tossing from side to side trying to shut up my mind. I hoped that I had not disturbed my husband's much needed rest. It was not that I loved him any less or was not more than concerned about his illness, it was only that I had found something that I loved in a way I could not even begin to describe. A craving, a deep yearning, something that I knew meant more to me than life itself.

The following Monday morning the first thing I thought of was my resignation and how I must get it to Frank Bravado, the school superintendent, immediately. I was sure he had heard of my husband's illness so my resignation letter would not come as a shock, rather something expected. After my arrival at work I began getting my thoughts in order. I sat at my computer and began what I felt was an appropriate letter of resignation. Upon completing it I noticed my printer was out of black ink. Fumbling through my drawers in search of some, I lifted my briefcase and instead of finding ink, the cover of the Tribune struck me first with horror then exhilaration. There on the front page was a huge photograph of Angie. Underneath was her name in big bold letters, ANGELA GREEN, a new voice in piano. The article went on to mention how she would be first featured, this week, at Carnegie Hall and listed some of the titles she would be performing. It also mentioned how she was on the rise to stardom and even went on to comment about her short stay at our High School. I must have read the article a dozen times. Perhaps, hoping that she had mentioned my name in some manner. At that very moment it became clear to me that I was going through with this outrageous plan. I knew that I was about to enter the biggest masquerade I could have ever envisioned. I knew it was wrong. Just what is it about someone that would be worth that trip to Hell? As I sat staring at Angie's smile I knew this was something I could not keep from doing. It would be the only way out of this slough of despond.

Carole Lenzy Daniel (Marlowe)

The fact was that I didn't care what happened to me. Satan had, with one stroke robbed me of everything that I lived for. There were other reasons, of course, but most importantly I wanted Angie! From the moment we held each other I felt bound to her. The urge to be with her grew with each passing day because it was only that which could make me want to go on living.

* * *

As I drove down Hunter Street I tossed words about as I was preparing what I would say to Frank. Even as I entered the Board of Education and made my way up the stairs to his office I still had doubts. Before I could have a seat his secretary ushered me back to his office while mentioning that he would be delighted to see me.

"Come in Ella, come in." His warm smile had always seemed to calm me in the most trying situations over the years. He reached for my hand and told me how nice it was to see me. Then with a solemn face he spoke softly almost apologetically. "Ella, words can not express the emotions I felt when I heard the news of Winston's illness. Seems like it was just yesterday that we were all out together at dinner or some function or another. It's just so hard to believe!"

"I know. I still feel as though it is all just a bad dream and that I am going to wake up at any moment." I said taking a seat opposite him.

"I can only imagine the terrible blow you must be experiencing. Mighty

Winston is what we use to call him when he beat us at some game or chess or something. He was always the strong one. It's just such a terrible thing." He spoke with a gentle tone, so soothing, something I had not realized I needed until now. "I suppose you will want to spend as much time with your husband as possible."

"Yes, of course, I feel it is something I must do. In all of the years we've shared together I can't seem to be with him enough during this time of illness." I said solemnly shaking my head, eyes downward.

"Ella, Please don't worry about anything. There is no problem. We have instructions from Northeastern that your replacement should arrive within the week." He said reassuringly. "As soon as I heard I got right on it. It's just our families have become so close over the years."

"I know. Thank you Frank for understanding and caring enough." I said rising. "You can't imagine how much this means to me." "You just take care of that man of yours while we will all be praying for a miracle." He said as we embraced. "Candy and I will stop over sometime if it won't be too much."

"No, please do stop over any time. Winston would love to see you both again, I'm sure. You are like family, you know." We embraced once more, he assured me of their love as I departed his office with one last wave good-bye.

* * *

Phillip Applegate arrived in Chicago the first week in April. He had flown straight from New York via the privacy of one of his father's private jets, which landed at Hatbox Airfield outside of town. Apparently, he had a limo awaiting his arrival and by half past noon, he stood smiling at me through our glass front screen door. He was accompanied by Ralph David, his pilot, and who also, as I learned later, was appointed his very own private pilot and chauffeur whom his father had handed down to him. I was a little disturbed by the repeated mention of Phillip's father. I spoke of it to my husband and he said, "He was never one to be thought of as less than Mr. Applegate! People of his affluence always seemed to hold a certain amount of tenure wherever their name might be mentioned." Seems his family had come into wealth through a chain of real estate. Apartment buildings, some high rises in New York City also

houses and commercial real estate."

"Like father, like son," I said brashly.

"I still don't appreciate him just

showing up here like this. Poor Jessica,

I know he broke her heart and I just

wonder how she could even stand the

sight of him after catching him like

that."

"People do forgive and forget Ella,"

Winston replied. "After all they do have

those two sons to raise and I don't

think Jessica is prepared to do that alone."

"Yes, but why wait until she had filed for divorce?"

"Now Ella, lets don't go poking our noses where they don't belong. We must have faith that our daughter will make the right decision for herself as well as for our two grandsons." I walked over and kissed Winston on the cheek. Now that he was nearly bedridden I kept very close to home.

Carole Lenzy Daniel (Marlowe)

I stood staring for a moment from one to the other through the screen door then suddenly caught myself. "Oh, where are my manners? Please do come in and be seated. Jessica will be in shortly. Lunch has been prepared if anyone is hungry." I said making my way to the kitchen. As Jessica and the boys entered the room Phillip caught her up in his arms and held her for what seemed like eternity. There was silence between them. Jessica did not protest. As a matter of fact I don't really know just who was holding on the tightest. Before releasing her they kissed very longingly. The sound of their lips together echoed through the air. As I reentered the room I found that our two guests had shed their jackets and were warming themselves near the cozy fire. The boys were just offering them sandwiches as I pushed Winston in his wheel chair near the couch where I was to be seated. I could tell that Jessica was caught up in the excitement, which pervaded the general atmosphere throughout the house. Even the two boys seemed to glow with some excitement. Not only because they were each wearing new suites for this special occasion but also, because this man was their father. As I watched how he held them each in one arm kissing each one on the cheek as If they had just been brought into this world I understood the magnitude of his power. He had complete control of his family and it was evident that he, by no means, was going to let anything get in the way of that. Noticing my husband's entrance he came right over and shook his hand in a manly yet gentle manner.

"It's good to see you again Mr. Whittington." "The news of your illness has reached my family and may I say that we are all in your corner. You can beat this and my father has agreed to offer any amount of money necessary to get you back healthy." He said releasing my husband's hand.

"Oh, I don't know if this is the kind of thing a person can just buy his way out of." "Although, I do appreciate your father's generosity, I wish it were that simple."

My daughter and I cleared away any remaining dishes after lunch and left the room allowing the men to talk. She incited the boys out with the promise of ice cream for helping. As we finished the dishes Jessica inquired of me as to whether she should go back to Phillip after everything that had happened.

"After the expression I saw on your face when he held you I would think you would be able to answer that question better than anyone." I said without meeting her eyes.

"Alright, I will admit that he has always held that power over me but I just don't know if I could ever forgive him for what he did." "Mom, I caught him with another woman!"

"I know honey", I said peering into her eyes, "It's never easy to make those kinds of decisions especially when

Carole Lenzy Daniel (Marlowe)

children are involved. You know him better than I ever could. Just how sincere he is would be something you have to ask yourself and if you're willing to find out." "Just because a person makes one mistake does not mean that they would repeat it."

She flung herself in my arms and whispered as a child might "Mom I love him so much"! "I want to be with him no matter what he has done", she sobbed. Then she stopped and looked me straight in the eye and said "Oh,

Mom what about Dad and his Illness? I could never leave his side at a time like this not even for Phillip. It is something I must pray over and await an answer from above."

I only smiled approvingly.

Jessica did leave. She had been unnaturally bright all afternoon but Winston, with his illness, did not notice. Phillip would only stare at her with something like affection. As soon as dinner was over we retired to our rooms. I knew that Jessica would want to talk. Considering her father's condition she would come to me possibly out of guilt. They had planned to leave at ten p.m. and around a quarter before the hour there was a knock at our bedroom door. I quickly answered it not wanting to arouse my husband who was by now fast asleep. We stood facing each other for a few moments. The night was still - not even the sound of the slightest breeze. Jessica laughed on a high note then she reached for me and held me tightly.

"Oh Mom," she said. "Thank you for everything. You will explain to Daddy for me won't you"? "I now know that I will be perfectly happy this time and, the boys, well the boys really do love their father and miss being with him. They really do need him in their lives". She paused for a moment; "We will come back to visit soon". Her hands were on my shoulders as she looked into my eyes, "I promise you," she said. "Please let me know immediately if there is any change in Dad's

Carole Lenzy Daniel (Marlowe)

condition". I promised her that I would.

"Good-bye Jessica". I said holding on to her as if she were fifteen years old going off to High School for the first time. "Write to us as soon as you get home".

"You know I will. Good-bye".

"Kiss the boys for us".

She was gone. I stood there for some time listening. I visualized her at home with her husband and sons where she belonged. I remained there a moment... listening to the sound of the car pull off and drive away until there was no sound at all. After which I returned quietly to our bedroom and tentatively into bed. Suddenly a feeling of desolation began to fill my heart, as I had never known before. I had thoughts of Angie. I fell asleep.

* * *

Within three weeks I was officially a retired High School Principal with nothing but time... Time to spend with my dying husband Winston who one month later desired to be hospitalized.

He was in such pain! On the night of my retirement party he really had given his all to be present and although he had to be wheeled in he had expressed his desire to be there by stating that he would not have missed it for the world. After my awards were presented he made a lovely speech about our marriage, our careers and about how we truly cared about the community and would go on caring for many, many years. It was painful for him to speak. Each word came with tremendous effort and sometimes force. Finally, he made it through and the crowd roared with applause. I was truly touched by the sentiment that was displayed there and could feel a tear rolling slowly down one of my cheeks. We were happy. We were together publicly again. We were accepted and applauded by all who knew and loved us. How could it all be taken away so abruptly?

Carole Lenzy Daniel (Marlowe)
* * *

After Winston was hospitalized I was left quite alone to watch myself growing older. Between visits to the hospital and the ladies and friends from the church who occasionally brought by lunch or a full dinner for me, I managed to keep myself somewhat busy. I would spend time at the church doing something, anything to make me feel that I was a part of some organization...that I was still a part of the living. In any case I knew that I was going into a new life. At that time I had no idea just what sort of life.

There was something uncanny about this. It seemed to be changing my character. At times I had feelings that I was already single. I began to notice that there was a new ruthlessness about me in a sinister sort of way. I was desperately lonely. I missed Angie and daringly one night set out to fill my yearning.

The club was as alive as I had remembered it the first time Angie had

Carole Lenzy Daniel (Marlowe)

taken me there. I had gone out just to

mingle, I told myself, just to be around

the living. I was having a good time

enjoying the music and all of a sudden

she appeared. The uniform is all I

remember about her and how totally

attractive she was. Before I knew it we

were in bed somewhere and her tongue

was as a snake slithering down my

throat as only Angie's had. Her

attractiveness made me wet with a

desire I had not felt in months. I

needed her so badly! As she took my

112

breath with her passionate kisses her

hand moved between my legs where my

pussy was soaked. She entered me with

first two fingers then three... I cried out

with pleasure as I came hard. Before I

knew it we were once again locked

together in passion. This time my

fingers tread up her thighs reaching

her awaiting, throbbing pussy where

they entered. Afterward I heard her

sweet moans until she finally came

with a loud cry of pleasure. We slept.

When I awakened She was nowhere in

sight. At first I thought I had dreamed the encounter but then remembered expressing to her from the start that I did not want to know her name and that she could never know mine, that I never wanted to see her again after that night. I remember lying there until late afternoon.

I visited Winston and that night cried myself to sleep. Was it possible that when someone died his soul could find refuge in someone else's body? There was a theory about that, I believed.

Somehow I felt that he would always be

with me. I felt I would never be

completely free of Winston. Those final

months passed as years. I took flowers to

his room until it could hold no more. It

was nothing like the excitement of

waiting for our wedding night 30 years

before. I remembered the comfort we

had derived from each other and the

lovely new feeling of security. I was far

from feeling that now. In fact, with

each passing day I was growing more

and more apprehensive. The house was

quiet, too quiet. I hated myself for what

I had done with that woman. I loved

what she did to me and how she did it.

We would share two more nights

together. I never knew her name.

* * *

Sometimes there was nothing I

enjoyed more than stretching out in

the big easy chair beside Winston's bed

and talking to him as if he were able to

respond. Once while in the middle of a

sentence I thought I saw him smile and

nod approvingly, after which a flood of

nurses and Doctors rushed in the room.

I was quickly ushered out. Dumbfounded, I heard myself screaming out "what's wrong?" Less than one hour later his Doctor came to the waiting room and told me that Winston had passed. They had done everything possible to keep him alive but to no avail. He had gone peacefully. I remember shedding so many tears there in the Doctors arms. I could not believe it. I was almost sure he had responded to my voice earlier with a smile. How could he be gone?

Someone other than myself must have made the funeral arrangements. All I remember was being at the funeral, dressed in black with the rain pouring and the tapping rhythm it made upon my umbrella. The Pastor's words were sweet and full of so many of the good things Winston was made of and had accomplished throughout his lifetime. His death was certainly a loss for his community as well as friends and colleagues and all that were touched by his caring nature. So many tears flooded my vision as I listened to the trumpets play as they lowered him into the earth. That one final glance of where he was being laid to rest was something that would remain in my memory forever. It was hard to leave. To just leave him there realizing that he would never return to our home again.

After the funeral, I have no idea how long I spent mourning alone in our bedroom. Jessica had asked me to come live with her in New York with she and her family rather than being left all alone to suffer. I had refused as I felt that without my Winston life would never be the same for me. There was a loneliness I could not shake. I had not anticipated that sort of grief. It was cold. It was constant. My only wish was to be left alone.

One night as I sat at the window in our bedroom, looking out at the moonlight, I wrote to Jessica. I enclosed a self-addressed stamped envelope for her response. Did her offer still stand? Did she and her family still want me to come and live with them for a while? Would it really be all right with her husband? I had made up my mind. I knew what I had to do in order to continue living.

Carole Lenzy Daniel (Marlowe)

Chapter Three

The Meeting

"Mom, Mom wake up! You must have been having a bad dream." I heard Jessica faintly say as she was shaking my shoulder gently.

Startled, I lifted my head from her shoulder and looked around dumb founded as to my whereabouts. "I must have dozed off." I said feeling the embarrassment of a child with his hand caught in the cookie jar.

"I'll say. You were asleep by the time I returned from the restroom. Which reminds me, I had better help you to the restroom. You have not gone since we departed Chicago."

"I had no idea you were keeping track of my restroom habits but since you are I guess we had better head that way. Even if I don't have to I'll make myself just for you."

"Good enough! Shall we go?" As Jessica pushed my wheelchair down the isle to the restroom located in the rear of the plane I noticed a young boy staring at me. He reminded me of one of my students who had attended Robinson High. He had taken notice of me getting on the plane and how I had to be seated.

"Does it hurt?" He asked wide-eyed but very sincerely.

"Not any more." I responded as she wheeled me past and into the restroom.

Carole Lenzy Daniel (Marlowe)

I noticed he was staring blankly at the bottom of my wheel chair as we made our way back to our seats. He watched carefully as I was helped out of the chair and placed comfortably into my seat. I avoided his eyes as his gaze worked its way up to my face. Finally, I allowed our eyes to meet as I smiled at him with a reassurance that it was really alright and that I was not in any kind of pain. He slowly returned my smile as if to express some sort of satisfaction or understanding as he was slowly approaching me with his hand outstretched as if to give me something.

"You dropped this back near the restroom door." He said, as his gaze softened somewhat. He opened his palm and released my broach into my hand. I stared at it for a brief moment.

"Thank you so very much. This means so much to me in a sentimental kind of way. Thank you for your honesty." I replied, in a meaningful tone. He grinned satisfactorily and skipped back

Carole Lenzy Daniel (Marlowe)

to his seat. Jessica whispered that he was such a nice boy. I agreed.

The plane whistled through the clouds as we settled back into our seats. I noticed Jessica had dozed off and after successfully satisfying the young boy's curiosity, I tilted back my head, opened my palm and stared at the beautiful broach.

* * *

The lights were the brightest things in the sky that night as I looked up at the sign, which read: In Concert Tonight,

The Other Side of Love

ANGELA GREEN, A New Voice in Piano! It was cold that evening as I shivered within the fur coat wrapped about me. Smoke seemed to smother our breath as everyone was huddled near the entrance trying to rush in. The Concert had been a sell out and we had been fortunate in getting tickets. Phillip had wanted the boys to study piano and had truly enjoyed Angela Green's music. He had not missed any of her concerts and I was afraid to ask just how he managed to come up with five front row seats at the last minute.

Silence fell over the Hall as the musicians quieted their instruments. There was a brief pause and then the thunder of an announcer's voice echoed throughout the room,

"Ladies and gentleman... I present to you the new voice in piano... Ms. Angela Greene!"

There was a standing ovation as the sound of applause thundered throughout the theater when she appeared. She looked magnificent in her jaded gown full of glitter and her smile seemed to add the finishing touches. She was truly beautiful. Her face was radiant as her eyes sparkled with sheer joy. She was graceful as she spoke, thanking the audience, then quietly taking her place at the piano as she named the title of her very first tune.

"I call this one Ella." She said, as she graced the keys gently. "It reminds me of times long past that were gentle yet long forgotten." There was silence and then the music began. It was a tender tune, which Angie played brilliantly. Throughout the Concert there was so much cheer and raves it became difficult to hear the announcement of a new song. The music was beautiful and her orchestra played as though they were accustomed to her style of piano playing. After nearly three hours of the greatest music I had ever heard played, Angie received a standing ovation as she made her final comments, blowing kisses as she exited

the stage. The applause were such that

she returned twice for bows and more

kisses. Then it was over. The orchestra

continued to play gently, quietly as the

exits became filled and the announcer

bid everyone a goodnight. I could see

from the expressions of my family's faces

that they had enjoyed the music with

the same amazement I had. We had

not moved as we were waiting for the

auditorium to clear as everyone was

single file towards the exits by rows.

"She is simply brilliant!" Phillip said with a look of satisfaction and enjoyment. "I've never heard anyone play as graciously as she."

"She was magnificent." Jessica added. "Well boys, did you enjoy the concert?" She asked lightheartedly. They each shook their heads in amazement and delight. "What about you Mom? Did you enjoy the music?"

"Very much so!" I said smilingly, then added. "You know, Angela Greene was a music teacher at our school before she became this great musical star."

"You mean you know her personally grandmother?" Billy asked in amazement.

"Of course I do," I replied. "Or at least I did at one time. I really don't know if she would remember me now or not... being the great star that she is and all."

"This is amazing!" Phillip added. "You mean Angela Greene was a teacher under you at Robinson High

Carole Lenzy Daniel (Marlowe)
and the two of you knew each other?

I'll bet that song, ELLA, was for you then."

I shrugged.

"Can we go and meet her Grandmother? Backstage and all?" the boys asked simultaneously.

"Oh, I don't even know if she would remember me now that she has become such a famous star." I replied. "When we knew each other she was merely a teacher with lots of dreams."

"Obviously those dreams came true for her." Jessica responded. "Just look at her now!" "It really wouldn't hurt to go backstage to try and see her, you know, she may just remember you after all and we can all get autographs."

"I don't know, it's been quite some time." I stammered.

"Ah, come on Mom!" Phillip insisted, "What could it hurt to try?"

They all stood there looking at me, beckoning me to do the unthinkable. Finally I gave in.

"OK, for all it's worth, let's go and meet this famous Ms. Angela Greene, if we are allowed to." I said turning in the opposite direction of the flow of the crowd headed to the parking lot. "Just don't be disappointed if she does not even remember me."

"We won't be." They all shouted as we all remained inside the Theater and made our way back stage.

There was a crowd standing, waving note pads and shoving to get past one another to a stage door with a star on it. ANGELA GREENE was printed in big bold letters below the star. The crowd seemed to be shouting something and anticipating, with much adrenaline, for the star to emerge. Slowly, the door opened and two men came out followed by someone dressed in an all white gown with ruffles on the outer edges. She had such a tiny waist line and a gorgeous face with a matching white wrap covering her head. She was smiling and blowing kisses to her fans in appreciation for their loyal support.

Carole Lenzy Daniel (Marlowe)

The crowd rushed toward her as the men encircled Angie and accepted the pads, one at a time, handing them to her while she signed each one with a big smile and a sense of urgency. We made our way closer as the crowd weaned. Jessica was fumbling with her purse, I suppose trying to find a pad or piece of paper to get an autograph.

"I know I have something in here to write on," she exclaimed, still reaching deep into the bag. She asked me to hold her check book, keys, and wallet while she managed to finally pull out a small note pad for which to get Angie's personal autograph.

"Ah yes. Here it is. I knew I had something to write on in here." She sighed.

"Thank God you found it!" Phillip exclaimed. "It would have been terrible to be this close to Angela Greene and not get an autograph because we couldn't find any thing to write on."

"I think I would have had her sign my arm and never wash it again." He giggled.

"Yeah right!" Jessica responded with a slight smile.

The boys had been too excited by the crowd to notice what was going on. Just as I was handing Jessica back her wallet, I glance up to see how close we were to the front of the crowd and at that moment our eyes met and locked on each other for what seemed like centuries. It was as if I was in a Trans.

All I remember is her bright smile and her lips forming the word Ella. I don't even remember if I smiled or not but a lump in my throat kept me from speaking and a feeling of sheer joy entrapped my limbs and kept me from moving. I felt Jessica remove the wallet from my outstretched hand and then they all seemed to be watching me.

I could not move!

I watched as Angie whispered something to one of the men before her. They seemed to glance in our direction and then started moving through the crowd toward us.

Suddenly we were standing face to face. I must have been blushing like some schoolgirl with a crush. She reached out and grabbed my hands, holding both of them into hers.

"Ella!" She cried. "It's been so long!"

Before I could respond she pulled me to her and we embraced for what seemed like hours. Those old feelings of our times spent together began to haunt me. After releasing me she smiled and said, "It's about time you came to see me. I just knew you would sooner or later, I just knew it!"

"Seems like you two are old friends." I heard from a voice behind Angie. The man stepped forward to stand beside her as she wrapped her arm into his.

"Darling, this is Ella, Ella Whittington, an old friend and ex boss. I don't know if you remember the principal at the school where I was working before I began my career. Ella, this is my fiancée Todd Baxter."

Carole Lenzy Daniel (Marlowe)

"Of course, I do remember." He extended his hand, which I shook graciously. "It's wonderful to see you again. And what, may I ask, brings you to New York?"

"My family." I smiled turning to my daughter and grandsons. "Angie, I don't believe you ever met my daughter, Jessica.

"No, never." She smiled and offered a warm hand. "Hello."

"It's so wonderful to meet you Ms. Greene. I'm... we are all huge fans."

Phillip offered his hand. "This is my Husband Phillip who, I might add, has never missed a concert of yours performed here in New York."

"Ms. Greene it certainly is a pleasure." Phillip was excited and smiling nervously. "I just can't believe I'm here shaking your hand like this. I truly enjoy your music. I have nearly all of your collections."

"I'm grateful." She spoke with a slight giggle. "Thank you so much for your patronage."

"By the way, these are our sons, Billy and Bradley, who are also fans."

The boys were bursting with excitement as Angie shook both their hands.

"It's wonderful to know that I have such young fans." She said.

"Ms. Greene, may we have your autograph?" Billy asked holding the pad and pen.

"Of course you may. It will be my pleasure." She took the pad, signed it, and wrote some comment underneath her signature.

"Darling, I do believe it is getting time for us to leave. It's getting late and we do have that little conference tomorrow morning, you know." Todd said reaching for her.

"Of course." She smiled up at him. She turned to me and said, "Ella, it's been wonderful seeing you again. We'll have lunch sometime and talk over old times."

"Sure we will." I reassured her.

Carole Lenzy Daniel (Marlowe)
"It's been great meeting your family. They are terrific. Thank you all so much for your loving support. Goodnight."

"It's been a pleasure." Todd added.

Goodnight!" We all called behind her as we watched her depart, nestled between the men surrounding her.

"Wow!" Billy shouted after they were out of sight. "I'll never wash this hand again."

"Me either." Cried Bradley.

Jessica looked at Phillip and smiling said, I know you're not going to agree."

"That makes three unwashed hands boys." He commented and we all chuckled.

The drive home was quiet. The boys had fallen asleep and all I could think about was her. "She looked absolutely stunning. She remembered me, which meant I did mean something to her after all. It was hard to think of her as engaged, though.

When was the wedding to be? I wondered if she was happy.

* * *

That night before falling asleep I thought of Angie and how it was before between us. Did she still have feelings for me? Could we ever again share what we had before she became this big star? I heard myself giggle out loud. "Why you old fool, Ella." I scorned. "That life for Angie is past and gone forever. How could she still have any intimate feelings for you?"

With that I fell into a restless sleep. I kept waking during the night thinking of Angie, seeing her face, as it was long ago when we made such passionate love. I had thoughts of the last night we'd spent together before her departure into the great unknown of the music world. I thought of how we held each other never wanting that moment to end. Then I awoke, startled. I remembered that face. The face of the man she now called her fiancée. That was also the face of the man who had spent that last night in Angie's apartment. The man I had watched leaving Angie in the wee hours of the morning. That was his face, Todd Baxter's face.

The Next morning I slept in late, not only because it was Saturday but also because I had not been able to sleep that night. I was awakened by a knock on the door. It was Jessica who brought in a late morning breakfast tray with a smile and ready for conversation.

"I made breakfast this morning as we all slept in later than normal. Thought you might be hungry." She said sitting in the chair beside the bed.

"Guess I am a little hungry, especially after all of the excitement last night." I yawned while sitting up. "Where are Phillip and the boys?"

"Phillip is meeting with friends at the golf course, for which he was late this morning, and the boys are out back, playing." She answered while placing the tray securely across me. She sat back into the chair then added. "We were all so exhausted from the excitement of last night, we found it hard to fall asleep."

"I know what you mean." I added.

"Mom, how well did you know her?" She asked, staring at me intently.

"We knew each other quite well." I responded, smiling slightly as I recalled our intimacy. "Although it was quite surprising that she did remember me, what with her fame and all." I took one bite of my toast. "I suppose fame truly does have its rewards. She really looked good, didn't she?"

"She looked absolutely stunning as she always has." Jessica replied excitedly. "Not to mention the concert. She was positively fabulous!" She added. "We shall never forget last night for the rest of our lives. "Can you imagine?" She asked dreamily. "Our standing this close to Angela Greene and getting personalized autographs?" "Not to mention the fact that my Mom knows her personally!"

Carole Lenzy Daniel (Marlowe)

"Did know her personally, mind you."

I responded. "I doubt we will ever see each other again. Stars do live very busy lives, you know."

"Yes, I do know." Jessica added. "But all the same, the fact is that you do know her and it will be exciting to mention it at the next office engagement Phillip and I attend." She giggled. "Can you imagine the envy?" With that she rose and waved a good-bye at the door as she left me to finish my breakfast.

I smiled as I took a bite of food and thought of how very wonderful it was, indeed, that Angie had remembered me. I wondered if she really meant what she said about our having lunch sometime. It would be nice to get together and talk about old times. After all, isn't that the real reason for my being in New York? I thought. Yes indeed, I did want to see her again. As a matter of fact, I was aching to.

Carole Lenzy Daniel (Marlowe)

* * *

Three months or so had gone by since the night of the concert. I had thoughts of Angie and our possible meeting again but reminded myself of the star she had become and that to her all I would ever be was an old acquaintance. I had all but given up on ever seeing her again, except in concert, when one Monday morning, as I was leaving for my usual weekly shopping, the telephone rang. Phillip and Jessica were at work and the boys were in school. Since I was in a hurry I did not stop to answer it. I thought, if it had been important enough, the caller would leave an urgent message or simply call back at a more convenient time. As I rushed out of the door I strained to hear if there was some sort of message being left. I heard nothing.

The streets were crowded, as they usually tended to be that time of morning. The hustle and bustle of people, movement and the constant traffic reminded me that this was truly New York and not the slower pace, more intimate home town I was familiar with. I had become somewhat accustomed to it, though, and seemed to find my way around quite well with the aide of an available map which I kept at my side at all times. As I walked down the familiar main strip of downtown passing all of the wonderfully decorated windows of all the major department stores, I stopped, as usual, in front of Saks to marvel at that diamond broach I had been admiring for months on one of the mannequin's coat. It was a white diamond encircled by smaller black ones, trimmed in gold. It was absolutely stunning! I was hoping to be able to purchase it before I attended Angie's next concert in the City. As I was standing there caught up in the beauty of it, I heard a familiar voice behind me say, "Hello Ella."

I thought I had imagined it so I did not bother to take my stare from the glitter of the diamond.

"It truly is very beautiful, isn't it?"

I looked up into the window and to my surprise, I saw Angie's reflection standing behind me. I whirled around in disbelief and there she was, smiling at me as if it were common that we should meet this way.

I opened my mouth but nothing came out. I finally heard myself crying "Oh my God! I don't believe it!"

She reached for both my hands and held them safe within hers and whispered, "please believe it. After meeting you and your family at the Concert I vowed to look you up. I hope you don't mind." She smiled that little girl smile I remembered so well. She was dressed in comfortable New York clothing. Blue jeans, with a large, hooded New York sweatshirt and jacket. She also wore sneakers and very dark shades, which covered most of her face. She lifted the shades slightly and

Carole Lenzy Daniel (Marlowe) peered deep into my eyes from below them.

"It's really you!" I shouted in disbelief. "Angie, it's really you!" We embraced for what seemed like forever all the while whispering how much we missed each other. Finally we parted and could only stand and stare at one another. I broke the silence.

"Would you like to have lunch? I know of a great place not far from here. We could walk even." My stare was deep into her eyes. There were so many questions I wanted to ask.

"I'd love to." She responded, then pulled me to her once more.

"Oh, Ella." She whispered close to my ear. "I've been waiting for this day for so long. "Somehow, I've always known we would be together again, some way, somehow."

She kissed my cheek and released me as we made our way through the crowded streets toward that restaurant.

We chose a table outside to dine. Angie remembered how I loved to watch the traffic, people and the hustle of a city while sharing a meal with someone. We both ordered the soup of the day and what was recommended to go with it. We sat quietly while we each finished our entrée then we both seemed to speak at once.

"So what have you been..." we each began. We laughed out loud simultaneously.

"You first." I said.

"No. You first. Age before beauty, you know." We each chuckled.

"OK, I suppose that's my cue." I replied straightening in my chair. "In that case, how have you been? And how are you enjoying being a celebrity, the famous Ms. Angela Greene?"

"Oh Ella, it's been like a dream come true for me. You know it was something I had always desired and knew I was capable of accomplishing under the right circumstances and with proper guidance. I love the lights, the fans and the opportunity to fill the world with my music. And Todd has been such a wonderful manager and promoter. He keeps us working and in demand, that's for sure." She replied excitedly. "As a matter of fact, I'll be opening in London in a few months. I'd love for you to be my special guest, Ella. That is, if you can get away for a week or two."

"London?" I shrugged.

"Please, just think about it for now. Six months or so is quite a while away."

She smiled. 'Besides let's enjoy what we have right here, right now. We're together now, Ella. Nothing will ever separate us again." She reached for my hand across the table and squeezed it. "Don't you feel it too?" She removed her hood and shades to look into my eyes.

The waitress interrupted before I could respond. As she was clearing our table and placing our dessert before us, she recognized Angie.

"Are you...you look like Angela Greene. Are you that famous concert

Carole Lenzy Daniel (Marlowe)

pianist? You are her! You are She!" She

screamed excitedly before Angie could

answer. "Can I please get your

autograph? I just love your music. I

think you are the greatest pianist,

ever!" She said nervously as she

scrambled through her apron pockets

for pen and paper. "Please, just sign this

napkin. And could you make it to

Mary? Oh, my family just won't believe

it!"

"Alright Mary, here you are." Angie

replied, smiling, handing her the

napkin and pen. "Thank you for being

a fan."

She walked away mumbling

excitedly, staring at the napkin as if it

held some magical words. "Thank you,

thank you." She said.

Angie and I burst out with laughter

but before we could get back into our

conversation a crowd began to form

around the table making a fuss over

Angie. They were all shoving, pushing

and screaming to get an autograph.

Angie complied and signed as many as

Carole Lenzy Daniel (Marlowe)

she could as we slowly made our way to

the street.

Thank God, Angie's limousine was

parked just outside the restaurant

where the driver stood with the door

opened as we pushed through the crowd

until we were safe inside. As the driver

pulled away from the curve and onto

the street, Angie reached for my hand

and squeezed it tight.

"That was a close call, huh ladies?"

The driver said while turning his head

174

half way towards the rear of the Limo where we were seated.

"Close call, indeed!" Replied Angie while rubbing my hand between each of her palms.

We drove for a half hour or so before stopping in front of the Le Grande Hotel where we exited and the driver mentioned Something to Angie regarding returning for us around eight or so.

"I have a surprise for you." Angie whispered close to my ear as we entered the luxurious Hotel. I followed quietly as we were shown to a lavish suite on the top floor.

* * *

"I've missed you Ella. You have no idea how I yearned for you after having departed Chicago. My dream was always that we would find each other again." She said, as she approached me reaching for both my hands. She caressed my temple clearing my hair from my eyes. "You're still so beautiful."

I looked up into her eyes which seemed to be laughing at me in some strange way. Her lips were turned upward at the corners in somewhat of an approving grin. Before I could respond I felt her lips press against mine. Her kiss was warm and soft as her tongue explored every inch of my mouth. I responded by returning every ounce of her passion. I felt my tongue penetrating the walls of her throat and beyond as her hand caressed my breast gently. I could have stood there kissing her forever at that moment. My knees would not have given out as long as I knew it was Angie I was holding and caressing.

"I want you Ella." I need your love as much as I always use to. You have no idea how I've longed for this moment." She whispered softly in my ear.

We finally parted and she began to undress. After removing her blouse she kissed me once more as I unsnapped her bra, removed it and tenderly allowed my tongue to explore the familiarity of her throbbing breasts. She moaned with satisfaction as her head was slightly tilted back and she exposed her breast, more readily, to my hungry tongue. Her hands slipped down to my trousers as she worked them down enough around my hips to allow her fingers to creep between my underwear and touch my now soaked pussy.

"Oh Angie!" I cried out passionately. "Only you can make me feel this way.

I've missed you so much! I need you so badly right now!"

My jeans had fallen down around my ankles as I was struggling to remove my blouse. Angie had completely undressed and was waiting for me under the covers in bed. After dropping my bra to the floor on the pile of other clothing, I climbed in bed beside her. We kissed, long, soft kisses before we made wild passionate love.

"I love you Ella." She said as I looked down into her eyes while my fingers explored the familiarity of her wet pussy. I drove into her as passionately as ever until she came with such force she let out a wild scream of satisfaction and lay exhausted beneath me. I kissed her neck, her chin, her nose and her lips for which she responded pleasurably.

"Will you lick me?" I asked in an almost whisper after I had rolled over on my back.

Before I was aware she was between my parted legs and I felt her tongue deep inside my throbbing womb. As she forced her organ in and out of my vagina and up between my swollen clitoris, I felt my drenched pussy drawing her in deeper and deeper.

"Don't stop Angie! Don't ever stop!" I cried out as I felt myself rising to a climax.

She continued to passionately fuck my pussy with her tongue until I came with such force it shook the bed. She rose just enough to kiss my navel and tease my lips with her moist tongue.

"Oh Angie" I breathed, as she fell limp beside me. I held her close to my breast in my arms, we both fell asleep.

We were awakened by a knock on the door and a man's voice informing us that our car was downstairs waiting. We must have been asleep for nearly four hours as it was now a little after eight.

"My God, Angie, look at the time!" I said rolling out of bed and quickly redressing myself. "My family is going to be worried about my where abouts.

I've never missed dinner."

Angie hurried to dress after which, we both exited the room nearly in full stride toward the elevator. The Limo was where we had left it as the driver held open the door for our entry. Before we parted Angie promised that she would be in touch soon. She whispered she loved me and we held each other once more. I felt good. I felt happy. I felt satisfied!

It was after nine when I entered the house, which was very quiet and already dark. I quietly made my way upstairs to my room with the hopes of not disturbing anyone if they had been asleep. After entering my room I quickly undressed, put on a robe and prepared to take a well-needed shower. As I was tying my robe around me there was a faint knock at my door.

"Mom, its Jessica. May I come in?" She called from beyond the door.

"Sure. Do come in, I am dressed." I replied, as I took a seat on the corner of my bed. The door opened and Jessica entered dressed in her nightgown and slippers with an inquisitive look on her face. She sat in the chair opposite me and took no time asking why I got home so late.

"I ran into a friend today." I answered somewhat nervously. "We had dinner and was talking and some how the time just slipped away." I reached for her hand. "You know I would have called had I realized it was so late. The last thing I would want to do is cause you and your family unneeded worry." I smiled.

She held my hand and said, "Mom, you're not a child and it is not necessary that you report in to us at all times. You do have freedom here, you know. You're not a prisoner. I merely came in to see if everything was alright and to tell you that we missed you at dinner." She looked deep into my eyes

Carole Lenzy Daniel (Marlowe)
then asked, "Was it someone you've known for a while?"

I released her hand, stood and walked over to my dresser to retrieve my bath items. With my back turned to her I replied, "Yes. It was Angie."

"Angie?"

"Yes. You know, Angela Greene."

"Mom, you had dinner with Ms. Angela Greene?" She asked in excited disbelief. "Angela Greene, the concert pianist, that Angela Greene?" She stood up.

"Yes, I did." I walked past her to retrieve some clean underwear from a different drawer.

"What? How? Where did you...?"

"We sort of ran into each other down town this afternoon."

"Angela Greene was downtown?" She asked with an unbelievable expression.

"Of course, however, she was dressed in somewhat of a disguise. Although, while we were having dinner a waitress did recognize her and we were nearly mobbed." I stood holding my bath

Carole Lenzy Daniel (Marlowe)
items. "We rode in her limo to a much more quiet location where we could really become reacquainted. We began conversing about old times and before I realized it, it was half past eight."

"How exciting that must have been! You and Angela Greene old friends like that." She exclaimed, hesitating at the door on her way out. "Were you very close friends?"

"I'll say. We were close enough." I replied with a chuckle. "By the way, she has offered for me to accompany her to her next concert, in London, in about six months or so. All expenses paid, of course."

"How exciting! Mom you must go!" Jessica replied excitingly. "We'll have to find just the right gown for you to attend as the special guest of the star." She re-entered the bedroom. "I know just the place we'll shop. It has the most exquisite gowns and women's fashion. You'll be a knockout. You wait and see. Then we'll have your hair done just so."

She continued misty eyed. "Oh, Mom, this is going to be so much fun."

"Yes, but I still have not decided whether or not I will accept Angie's invitation. I would be away at least a week, you know."

"So."

"So, I just need time to think about it." I replied as I eased past her heading down the hall toward the bathroom. "We can speak on this issue another time. Right now, I'm tired and would like to shower and get some rest."

"Alright, but you can be sure that I will be doing my best to persuade you to go." She said as she turned the opposite direction toward her bedroom. "Goodnight Mom."

"Goodnight."

That night I lay awake thinking about the events of the day. The meeting with Angie, how we ended up in bed together and why. Was it a chance meeting? Had Angie known previously that I frequent that area of downtown? Had she seen me there before today? Perhaps following me to learn of my routine? I tossed and tried to sleep but my mind was still wide-awake with all sorts of questions.

Could she still possibly be in love with me as she had professed? What of her Fiancée? How could she make love to me the way she had that afternoon, then face the prospect of marrying someone she obviously does not love? I questioned my own feelings. Had I regretted sharing those passionate moments with Angie? Of course not! I was more excited than I had been when we were together before she became a superstar. And now, the prospect of being with Angie again was more than just exciting. It was comforting to feel her love for me in ways that only her touch could make me feel. I was beyond excited!

* * *

The days passed quickly as Jessica and I anticipated Angie's call. A week had gone by, then two. There was still no communication from Angie after nearly two months. We had all but given up, as I was sure Jessica had even forgotten about the ordeal entirely. I, too, was beginning to wonder if I had, in fact, fabricated Angie's exact words to me regarding her concert in London.

After four months had passed since our meeting, my home life was pretty much back to normal. School was out as it was nearing time for the family summer vacation and the boys were anticipating it with the utmost excitement. Phillip had expressed wanting to visit the Grand Canyon this year, then head to California for another week at Disney Land. I had been reluctant to go this summer and was finally confronted by Jessica who showed concern about my anti vacation attitude. On the evening before their departure she came to my room to inquire about my reluctance.

Carole Lenzy Daniel (Marlowe)

"Mom, I just don't understand why you would want to stay here alone while we are out enjoying the summer weather and seeing different parts of the Country. Phillip, I and the boys would do nothing but worry about you." She said solemnly, as she sat across from my bed in the big easy chair.

"Jessica, you can all rest assure that I will be alright here alone. I need some time to myself and am really looking forward to having the place to myself for once. Don't worry, I won't have any wild parties or have the place in shambles when you return." We both laughed. "Go and enjoy your family vacation and leave this old woman here, this time. "I'll look after things and possibly get some serious reading done. I do appreciate your offer though, as usual." I said, facing her.

"Well, only if you're sure Mom. You know, we'll be gone a month or so."

"I know. And it will be good for you to spend time together as a family without my being along." "Something

you have not been able to do since I

arrived. So go on. I insist. I am still

very capable, you know." I smiled. She

stood and mentioned something of my

seeing them off early the next morning,

around six. I gave her my word that I

would.

Excitement rang high in the boy's

voices as they were preparing for their

trip. Phillip and Jessica were excited as

well. It was half past six before the last

piece of luggage was placed in the van.

The boys had claimed their seats and were in them with seatbelts latched. They were waving to me through the windows.

"Goodbye Grandmother, don't get too lonely." They called out. "We'll send post cards from every town we visit."

"I would appreciate that very much." I called back from the front door. "Don't forget to write me a note on each one about all of your wonderful adventure."

Jessica and I embraced as Phillip stood for his goodbye kiss on the cheek. "We'll miss you this time." He said as he was stepping back.

"You all go on and have fun." I replied. "Be sure and drive safely." To my surprise, the boys had jumped from the van and were clinging to me with tears in their eyes. "We'll miss you Grandmother." I gave them each a shallow kiss on their cheek, assured them that it would be alright, then stood and watched them wave from the back of the van as they were driving away. I stood waving until well after they were no longer in sight then returned to my room and planned what I would do my first day home alone.

* * *

It was early afternoon when I found myself, once again, at the storefront marveling at that broach through the window. The clerk inside waved to me and motioned for me to come inside and have a look around. She indicated that it would be much better, my being

able to actually touch and hold the

item I was admiring. I smiled back in

such a way to let her know that I had

no intentions of entering the store and

as I turned to walk away I felt a hand

on my shoulder. I heard a soft voice

whisper, "Ella." I spun around and

there stood Angie smiling like a young

schoolgirl with a crush on an older

teacher.

"I was hoping I might find you here."

She said, still smiling.

"Angie! What a surprise and where on earth have you been?" I exclaimed. We embraced for a brief moment as I enjoyed the smell of her hair and the tenderness of her body next to mine. "I've been so worried after not hearing from you for so long." I released her.

She stared deep into my eyes in a sad sort of way, then said "Ella I don't have much time now to talk, my car is waiting for me. I'm due at a meeting in half an hour. I came here hoping to find you to ask you if you would meet

Carole Lenzy Daniel (Marlowe)

with me later this afternoon, say around four? I could send my car for you to bring you to the Hotel. I will explain everything then. Please say yes. I could have my driver pick you up at half past three." She stared at me intently.

I studied her expression before responding, "of course, I would love to meet with you this afternoon." I said. "Does your driver know where to retrieve me?"

"I know everything about you, lady."

She reached out for my hands. Pressing my palm against her cheek she whispered, "I'll be waiting for you Ella. See you soon."

I stood for a moment watching until she was no longer in sight. I looked down at my watch, which read one thirty. I hurried along home, not thinking about those items that I had come to town for, but only of her. Angie was back. And I was about to burst with excitement!

Carole Lenzy Daniel (Marlowe)

It was exactly four p.m. as I entered the Hotel and was in the elevator heading for Angie's suite. I was thinking of how I had taken time to shower and dress for her. I wore a White, sleeveless vest with stunning white matching britches and sandals to match. I thought I looked rather appealing with my baby blue eyes amidst my blond, streaked graying hair. My figure was still in tact and I wondered if Angie appreciated it.

She was asleep as I sat on the corner of the bed looking down at her. My god, she was so beautiful! Her tanned skin was a perfect light brown and she looked like a princess awaiting a Prince to kiss her before she could awaken. I gently caressed her hairline and cheek with the back of my fingers as I bent slowly to kiss her lips gently.

"Angie," I whispered. "It's Ella. I'm here."

She slowly opened one eye, then whispered, "Oh Ella, you've come."

Carole Lenzy Daniel (Marlowe)

I shook my head then bent to kiss her once more. It was a long, tender kiss and before I knew it my fingers had found their way between her legs to her wet, hot pussy. She was naked under the covers as she drew me down to her and fumbled with the buttons on my vest. My fingers were inside her and my lips were wrapped around her warm breast. I sucked gently as she removed my vests and her breath was hot upon the back of my neck. My fingers moved violently in and out of her womb as she moaned with satisfying pleasure in my ear.

"Don't stop! Don't ever stop!" She cried with pleasure. "Oh Ella, I've thought of no one but you and the way you make me feel. You're so gooooood to me!" She came with grunts and groans. We laughed out loud as she hurried my pants down below my buttocks then off my ankles. I crawled into bed with her as I came prepared not wearing a bra or panties. We kissed passionately, my tongue exploring the familiarity of her mouth. Her palms held a cheek of my

Carole Lenzy Daniel (Marlowe)

buttocks in each one, squeezing softly yet firm enough for me to feel. We parted lips as we lie facing one another. I took her chin in my hand and told her how I missed her and thought I would never see her again.

"You're never getting rid of me again, ever." She exclaimed. "I love you Ella. I really do love you."

With that she held my breast in her palm and tenderly made love to my nipple. Licking gently then taking it all inside her mouth. I moaned gently as

212

she softly sucked my breast while her fingers had found my drenched vagina. We enjoyed that moment of passion as I moved my body to accommodate the movement of her fingers. I kissed the top of her head as her tongue worked my breasts. Alternating from one to the other until my climax came with sheer harmony and satisfaction.

Exhausted, we each fell back on the bed, breathing heavy yet enjoying the thrill of all we had enjoyed. There was

Carole Lenzy Daniel (Marlowe)

silence for a few moments as we stared

at the ceiling above until I reached for

Angie and pulled her close to me.

Wrapping her in my arms, I told her

how much she meant to me and that I

did not know how I managed to get

through those times without her. She lie

quietly for a while until she caught her

breath.

"Ella, I wanted to tell you that I had

to leave town on an emergency, that's

why I had not contacted you since we

saw each other last." She sighed. "I had

a Concert to do that I had not prepared for at all. It was sort of a last minute thing, in Paris, that Todd had not mentioned to me until the very day we were to depart. You can imagine how devastated I was learning of it at the last moment and not having any time to prepare. I also wanted to call you to let you know what had come up but did not get to." She looked up into my eyes as I held her cheek to my chest. I kissed her forehead and assured her that nothing she could not control would ever have any effect on my love for her.

"We were meant to be. Don't you know that by now?" I asked, rubbing my chin against her hair.

"I've always known it. From the very beginning, I knew our love would break barriers and go beyond the dimensions of what is considered normal." She held me even tighter around my waist. "I just don't understand why a love such as ours could not ever be accepted as normal

216

within society. I mean, we would be together forever. Death would be the only thing ever to separate us and yet, our love has been condemned by a society of people who merely wink at true love. A society of men who seem to feel that love can be all of the things they choose to engage in sexually, whether with multiple wives, little children, or young boys. Even having adulterous affairs outside of their marriages, as well as other things. Yet our kind of love, the other side of love, is heavily criticized and condemned, even cursed." She responded with anger in her voice. "How can such a beautiful thing be regarded as something so terrible?"

I held her even closer to me as I responded.

"Nothing is neither good or bad but thinking makes it so. Our love can be whatever we make of it. Successful love is what we want to share. An endless love, one that will surpass the test of time. Just look at what it has endured already. We're together now when the odds were against our ever seeing each other again."

She smiled, "yes, we are together again, forever this time."

Once again, silence filled the room as we enjoyed the feel of each other's softness. I had nearly dozed off as I felt Angie wiggle out of my arms to get out of bed.

"Ouch!" She cried.

Carole Lenzy Daniel (Marlowe)

"What is it? What's wrong?" I asked,
lifting my head to see her walking
toward the bathroom.

"Oh it's nothing. I have a slight
bruise on my shoulder which I bumped
as I was getting out of bed." She called
back to me.

"You should be more careful." I
replied. "How can you see anything?
It's dark in here. Where are the lights?"

"I don't need any lights to find all of
your hot spots." She replied with a
chuckle as she climbed back into bed.

"I could find them all with a blindfold on. She raised herself on one arm to look down into my eyes.

"Do you really think you know them all?" I asked smiling. "Show me."

With that I pulled her gently down on me as our lips met tenderly, passionately. We toyed with each other's tongue as our lips stayed hard pressed together. Our lovemaking was soft and tasteful as we both came easy, almost too easy.

Carole Lenzy Daniel (Marlowe)

"Told you so." She whispered softly

into my ear.

I smiled.

Chapter Four

London

It was half past ten as I turned the key in the lock to open the front door at home. The house was dark and felt very empty. I clicked on the light switch and made my way to the kitchen for some warm tea. After neatly placing the kettle of hot water over the open flame and preparing a cup filled with a tea bag, I sank down into one of the chairs, breathed a long sigh and waited for the whistle. I thought a great deal of the events of the evening. How being with Angie had not seemed any different. As a matter of fact, it felt even more right. Right or wrong, all I knew was that I was going to continue being with her, come hell or high water, and it would not matter whom, if anyone and everyone found out about it.

That night in bed I lay awake thinking about some of the things she had mentioned. I tried to recall every moment of our time spent together. Why would she want to take me to London with her? Surely she was aware of the tension it could create for me being her guest along side her fiancée.

* * *

The days passed quickly. A week had gone by until one morning around noon I was awakened by the ringing of the doorbell. I sat up for a moment before grabbing my robe and heading downstairs to answer it. "One moment please!" I shouted, hoping whoever was there would not leave. After peering out, I opened the door and was greeted by a man in uniform with a large package placed at his feet.

"Good afternoon Ma'am. I have a package here for an Ella Whittington." He said smiling.

"I am she." I responded.

"Would you please sign on the dotted line?"

He handed me an envelope then lifted the package and asked where I would like it.

"Please just right inside here." I pointed to the entrance. Thank you."

"You have a good day." He smiled and was gone, closing the door behind himself. I stared at the package for a long moment then decided to read the note before attempting to open the box. I walked past it and into the living room where there was a letter opener on the table. After opening it a ticket fell out and there was a note inside with the name, Angela Greene, as the letterhead. The note read:

My Dearest Ella,

Here is the ticket I promised. Please accompany me in London, for one week, as my special guest during my concert. At no expense to you, you shall be required to stay at the BaRitz Hotel with transportation to and from the Concert Hall each night of the performance. I am also sending a selection of clothing I would love for you to wear along with a special gift I have included just for you. I will be looking forward to seeing you there. Your plane ticket has the dates of your departure and return listed on it. A limo will await your arrival in London to drive you to the Hotel. Hope to see you soon.

Angie

I read and re-read the note until I finally decided I would open the package. Of course, I had decided that I could not take Angie up on her offer as the family was away and would not return for another three weeks or so and someone had to stay and look after things. I reminded myself that I had volunteered to do just that, as I was opening the box. Besides, how could I just leave like some carefree teenager blinded by love? There was a handsomely wrapped box sitting on top of a multitude of clothing, which caught my eye. As I was opening it I wondered just what sort of gift Angie thought I would like. As I removed the last bit of paper and slowly opened the

box, I caught up my breath as it was

the very diamond broach I had been

admiring through the window at Saks

the first time Angie approached me. It

was stunning! The white diamonds

with black trimmed in gold was

absolutely gorgeous. Engraved on the

back was:

To Ella, with all of my heart forever!

Angie.

I held it close to my heart and with

tears in my eyes proceeded to go

Carole Lenzy Daniel (Marlowe)

through the box, taking the clothing

out, piece by piece. They were some of

the most exquisite gowns I had ever

seen. I tried them all on and each one

seemed to be even more stunning than

the one before. They all fit perfectly, too.

I smiled as I was trying on the final

piece. I thought of how Angie had said

she knew me better than I knew myself.

I now was absolutely convinced that

she did.

I spent the next few days pondering over the trip and how I could spend a week in London and still care for my responsibilities at home. I wondered if I should mention it to my daughter when they called from their vacation or simply go and return before their summer trip ended. I had made up my mind that I would simply leave a note explaining my whereabouts and exactly when I was scheduled to return. After all, Jessica and I had decided that I should take advantage of Angie's offer long ago. Wasn't it she who had demanded that I go at all costs? Hopefully, my week spent in London would end before their return and I would not have to explain anything about the trip at all. My mind was made up; I was going to accept the offer. Could I dare turn down any opportunity I had to be with Angie? I knew that I could not.

* * *

My plane arrived in London around two-thirty, the following Friday afternoon. There was a limo awaiting my arrival, just as Angie had informed me would be. As I was preparing to check in at the front desk I heard someone yelling from a dark corridor on the opposite side of the hotel. As the voice became clearer and the person ran out of the darkness, I could see that it was Angie.

Carole Lenzy Daniel (Marlowe)

"Ella, you made it! You're here!" She cried, with her arms stretched out ready to receive me.

"Of course I'm here! You didn't think I would turn down an opportunity to be a special guest of the great Ms. Angela Green, did you?" I chuckled as we held each other close. "I missed you!" I pressed hard against her and thought for one, slight second that I felt her wince as thought she were in some kind of pain.

"It's good to see you, Ella. I'm happy you came." She smiled, attempting to shrug off the pain.

"What! And have to return all of those beautiful gowns? Not to mention that gorgeous broach, Angie you shouldn't have!"

"Yes, I should have!"

We held each other at arm's length. "Then I'll wear it every night of the concert and always keep it close to my heart to remind me of you and your kindness."

"Precisely the point!" She smiled warm into my eyes and I thought I felt my heart skip a beat or two. We stood staring for a moment until we were interrupted by a deep voice that sounded vaguely familiar.

"Ah, there you are! I've been looking all over for you. You're needed at the hall for suggestions on lighting and positioning of the piano. Darling, you know you should always stay around the hall until we get things properly set up. Why must I run to find you as if you were some child at play?"

Angie held her head in shame and through unhappy eyes said, "Todd, honey, this is Ella. Remember my old friend from Chicago? I believe the two of you became re-aquatinted at the concert in New York."

"I don't..." His eyes swung around barely to meet mine.

"Of course, I remember your fiancée." I quickly responded. "What a pleasure to see you again."

He took hold of my extended hand.

"Yes, of course Ella, yes I do remember."

"So you see darling why I had to escape the concert hall? I wanted to be at the hotel when she arrived. As my invited guest, I wanted to personally make sure that she found her room safely and that she were being treated with the utmost kindness." Angie's eyes avoided his as she spoke.

"Yes, but you know..." Todd began rather harshly.

"It's alright Angie." I interrupted. "I'm grateful for everything you've done so far but please don't let my arrival keep you from your duties. I do understand. There will be plenty of time, possibly later, that we can spend together talking over old times. Besides, I'm sure I can handle everything from here." I spoke calmly. "It's just great making your acquaintance once again, Todd." I shook his hand once more while throwing my bag across my shoulder. "Make sure she delivers a

Carole Lenzy Daniel (Marlowe)

wonderful performance tonight." I glanced toward Angie.

"Of course she will." He replied, releasing my hand.

"It will be an encouragement for me just knowing that you are in the audience, Ella." Angie smiled. "Hope we can at least share a drink after the concert."

"I'd like that."

We embraced quickly then I watched until she and Todd were no longer visible in the hallway.

The hall smelled of lilac and the stage was superb. I was greeted at the door and seated appropriately by an attendant. I felt quite comfortable dressed in the jade gown and matching shoes I had selected from the wardrobe Angie had provided for me. The broach fit along perfectly with my other jewelry selection for the evening. I was seated opposite the stage with a direct view of the piano and the orchestra. There was a giant poster of

Carole Lenzy Daniel (Marlowe)

Angie above the piano, which read,
"Angie! A new voice!" The orchestra
played a soft, gentle melody as the
constant chatter of distant voices
became louder as the concert hall
began to fill. I was amazed at the well-
dressed crowd and how Angie's music
even appeared to attract the younger
generation as well. As I was staring
into the crowd I heard a familiar voice
call my name in somewhat of a
whisper. After turning in the direction
of the sound, I was surprised to be

staring straight into the eyes of Todd,

Angie's fiancée. Apparently, he was to

be seated right next to me.

"How wonderful to make your

acquaintance once again, this

evening." He was smiling and reaching

for my hand.

"It's good to see you again."

"She's certainly turned out quite a

crowd opening night. I certainly hope

this continues through out the week."

He released my hand.

Carole Lenzy Daniel (Marlowe)

"Angie plays so beautifully. I'm sure the audience will find her music quite delightful and return for more."

His deep blue eyes seemed to be studying me. He looked as if he were going to respond but was interrupted by the drastic change in the sound of the music being played by the orchestra.

"Ah, it's nearly show time." In a most positive gesture he motioned for me to take my seat first, then sat with every bit of his enthusiasm fixed on the stage.

A smile lit up his face as the lights gradually grew dim and the music became louder and more fierce. He seemed to be giving his approval in some sly manner as the spotlight beamed in on the piano, then on the announcer, who stood in the corner of the front row of the orchestra and announced, with great admiration and force:

"Welcome ladies and gentlemen!" The crowd grew silent. He continued, "Tonight, for her first appearance ever

Carole Lenzy Daniel (Marlowe)
at the Palladium, I bring to you, Ms.

ANGELA GREENE! The wonderful new

voice in piano!" The crowd roared as

the curtain began to open and finally

there awaiting her cue, stood Angie.

Brilliantly dressed in the glitter of

diamonds and the lavender gown she

wore to offset the colors on stage and of

the orchestra, she seemed ominous. The

crowd's cheers were so loud the sound of

the orchestra was drowned out. I could

not even hear myself clapping. After

bowing and blowing kisses into the

crowd, she walked slowly toward the piano, curtsied once more, then sat gently on her bench. The orchestra was silent. She positioned herself comfortably then began playing a soft melody nearly to a whisper. Then she spoke. "Hello everyone!" The crowd responded with a gentle applause. She continued, "For my first selection I would like to share a tune with you I wrote while being inspired by a most wonderful and dear friend." The orchestra began slowly, but gently to creep into the melody. "I call this one "Ella," hope you enjoy it as much as I do." There was a pause in the music, and then Angie began a tender roll on the piano after which the orchestra joined in producing a tantalizing melody with the piano leading the song. She played wonderfully! The sounds blended so well together the music would move even her most harsh critic to praise her. After a passionate ending, the crowd roared as she stood and waved her arms toward the orchestra. There was even a standing ovation for nearly five minutes after she sat down again to begin a new tune. All evening, after every selection, there was a standing ovation with whistling and applauding so loud; a pause preceded every tune. The concert ended the way it had began with Angie exiting the stage exactly as she had entered it. The crowd went wild as she curtsied and blew kisses out among them. The roar continued long after she had made three or four encores.

Carole Lenzy Daniel (Marlowe)

Even after the announcer stood to wish all a goodnight and reminded everyone of the concert continuing the following night and every night, for one week. Someone screamed out Angie's name and finally the exits began filling with fans leaving the hall. It was noisy still as the announcer mentioned that Ms. Greene would only sign autographs her final evening. The orchestra continued playing until security gave the word that the building had been secured and the last

of the fans had left the parking lot.
Then, one by one they filed off the stage
to prospective rooms where they stored
their equipment and changed into
more casual clothing.

"Shall we go and see how our
wonderful star is doing after that most
brilliant performance?" Todd asked
after watching the last orchestra player
leave the stage.

"I'd love to." I responded taking his
arm as we started back stage toward
Angie's dressing room.

Carole Lenzy Daniel (Marlowe)

Before we could open the door she appeared outside it and Todd took her up into his arms, kissing her cheek.

"You were fantastic tonight darling!" He said, holding her close to him. "I'm sure we had a sell out. I'll have to get the actual count later." He kissed her lips tenderly and as they parted she looked over at me with a different sort of expression.

"Ella!" She smiled, reaching for my hands. You look so beautiful. I hope you enjoyed the concert. I'm really looking forward to speaking with you at the party later." She squeezed tenderly.

"Thank you." I replied, returning her squeeze. "I enjoyed every moment of it! And yes, you were simply brilliant. I can hardly wait for tomorrow night's performance. I'll be hearing those tunes in my sleep."

"Now that's the kind of response we would like to hear from all of the fans that were present tonight. We certainly hope they are all anticipating another performance." Todd, interrupted,

Carole Lenzy Daniel (Marlowe)
reaching for Angie. "Darling we must get to that after party. So many are awaiting our arrival you know."

"Of course. Ella won't you ride with us to the party? After all, it is at the hotel where we are staying and we are all headed the same direction."

Todd Sighed.

"I'd be delighted to." I responded. "Only, of course, if it is alright with your fiancée."

With all eyes on him, Todd gave another sigh then responded rather sarcastically. "It's perfectly alright with me if that's what Angie would like.

"Then it's settled because that is what I would like." Angie smiled, then grabbed my arm as we headed toward the exit and the limo.

The ride to the hotel was quiet as Angie sat next to me, opposite Todd. She held my hand and squeezed it on occasion to let me know how happy she was that I had been able to come to London to be with her. I was happy too.

Carole Lenzy Daniel (Marlowe)

Just being in London. Just being with

Angie!

Our arrival at the hotel was met with

much chaos and distraction. As we

were exiting the limo we were met with

numerous cameras and reporters

fighting to get to Angie.

"Ms Greene, how do think your first

concert in London went over?" One

would ask.

"Do you have any regrets about any

part of your performance tonight?"

Asked another.

"Can we expect wedding bells between you and your manager any time soon?" Still another asked.

"How long will the show run in London?" Lights were flashing as Angie sank quietly between Todd and her bodyguards fighting to enter the hotel. She yelled a few answers toward the media, along with a nice smile and yet hurried along to be free of the questions and cameras. Once inside she smiled at me and commented that the Media was the part she thought she would love the most but found that she

despised it's intimate look into her

personal life and the publication of

every little detail of her past history.

"I've heard of freedom of the Press

before but, can they really do that?" I

asked. "Can they really storm on you

like April showers and expect you to

comment about personal things in your

life after a full evening of work?"

"You just don't know Ella! Oh, the

stories I could tell you about the Press.

Some of them will do anything for a

story. And I do mean anything! Even going so far as to snoop outside your home taking pictures of you from a distance and publishing them with not so true stories. Anything to sell a magazine today, even if it's half the truth."

The crowd had thickened somewhat and the hum of voices began to get louder. One of the caterers approached us with drinks on his cart and offered us each a drink. We both took one and just as we were beginning to get comfortable with each other, Todd appeared.

"Oh darling, there you are once again with Ella. There are some very important people here tonight who would very much love to set up a personal interview on television with you. Come, I'd like to introduce you." He grabbed her arm and directed her to the opposite side of the room. As they departed he looked back at me and smiled. "Won't you please excuse us Ella? Angie has some business to attend to. As a matter of fact, she may be quite tied up all night."

As they disappeared into the crowd, I finished my drink, held a couple of conversations with individuals who found themselves speaking of how much they had enjoyed the concert and how they believed Angie to be the greatest concert pianist who ever lived. I truly believed that as well. More importantly, I believed she was one of the most sensitive and loving creatures who ever lived. I knew her like that and felt some pride in assuring myself that I, alone,

knew her from a different perspective. I

knew her from an intimate one!

* * *

It was nearly three a.m. before I

reached my room and fell helplessly

into bed and passed out. After I don't

know how many drinks or

conversations, I somehow managed to

excuse myself, find my room and crash.

I have no idea how long the party

lasted only that I was awaked around

five a. m. by loud shouting and thuds

on the walls of my room. I could not quite make out the voices or the words but, could clearly hear someone being tossed against furniture or something and the roar of the man's voice as he shouted, what sounded like obscenities at a woman who seemed to be weeping yet yelling back in some sort of defense. I could hear the rage within his voice and what sounded like thuds of physical violence. I rolled out of bed to listen, then placed my ear to the wall to try and make out words being shouted.

Carole Lenzy Daniel (Marlowe)

I wondered if I should call the police?

Surely others must have been awakened by the noise. Did this sort of thing happen in this hotel often?

"Someone had better do something before he kills her." I whispered. I glanced around the room then at my reflection in the mirror only to find that I was still dressed in my clothes I had worn to the concert and party the previous evening. I then peeked out of my door to see if anyone else had been awakened as I had by the noisy argument and fight occurring in the room next to mine. I closed the door and wondered if I should report this to the front desk.

"I could call." I thought.

Just as I had lifted the receiver to my ear I noticed the arguing and noises had suddenly stopped. It was now quiet and I could not help but wonder if he had killed her. I returned to the wall to place my ear against it once more. It was silent, as if nothing had ever gone on in the room beyond this wall. I paced a while still wondering if there had been a murder committed and whether or not I should report what I had heard. I lay back on my bed staring at the ceiling. Finally, I convinced myself that whatever had happened in that next room was none of my business and if there truly had been a murder the authorities would find out soon enough.

I must have dozed off for when I awakened it was already time to dress for an evening at the concert hall to enjoy another night of Angie's music. I had made up my mind that I would not attend another after party, as I was much too tired the previous afternoon. Not only had I not seen as much of Angie as I would have liked but lacked the energy to get out and see some of London as well. I was startled by the ringing of the phone as I put on the last of my jewelry and was adjusting my broach through my reflection in the glass.

"Yes." I answered.

Carole Lenzy Daniel (Marlowe)

"Ms. Whittington, your limo has arrived." The desk clerk's deep voice sounded loud and clear.

"Thank you. I'll be right down." I briskly grabbed my wrap and rushed out of the door toward the elevators. As I past the door of the room next to me, memories of what I had heard earlier that morning brushed through my mind. I walked slowly past hoping to see someone, anyone who might be staying in that room so as to have some idea whether or not I had imagined it all. The door remained closed as I continued to stare at it from inside the elevator. On the ride down, I reminded myself that whatever happened, if anything at all, was none of my business and I would put it out of my mind.

* * *

I was awakened that night in terror! I sat up in bed as a loud scream penetrated my sleep. I looked around the room to remind myself of where I was and glanced at the clock on the

271

table next to the bed. It was 3 a.m. I crawled out of bed to place my ear to the wall to hear if the scream had come from the same room as the night before. All I could make out were muffled voices, that of a man's and a woman's. After a few moments there was silence. I continued to listen for a half-hour or so then sat in the chair opposite my bed. I recalled the events of the evening and how brilliantly Angie had performed. I had enjoyed her performance so well that I did attend the after party after all. I somehow knew that it was important to Angie that I attend. As usual, Todd continued to keep Angie near him and with others, I supposed who were important to her career. I mingled and enjoyed myself until I decided to retire to my room, once again, without being able to say goodnight to Angie.

After an hour or so of quietness from the room next door, I returned to bed and that afternoon decided that I would get out and roam the streets of

Carole Lenzy Daniel (Marlowe)

London. I did and enjoyed myself. There were so many nice shops and sidewalk café's I nearly forgot about the time. As I rushed through the crowded streets, all I could think of was that I must attend that concert. After all, that was the reason I had been invited to come to London. I was grateful. I would not let Angie down, nor would I allow anything to keep me from attending.

What a brilliant performance Angie put on that night. For the first time, she smiled and winked at me during one of her intervals. I sat with a slight smile in return not wanting Todd to acknowledge my sheer excitement during the remainder of the concert. As usual, it was a huge success. The Hall buzzed with cheers and screams at which Angie returned to the stage for three encores. The crowd had been so that there was standing room only, which now filled the exits. I had decided that I would retire early this evening and this time not attend the after party. The events of the day had me lacking for energy and I did intend to return to the streets of London the following afternoon. I avoided going back stage and followed the crowd through the exits to where my limo had remained each evening after every concert.

"Attending the party this evening ma'am?" The driver asked as he held open my door until I was comfortably in my seat.

"Not tonight." I replied trying to sound exhausted. "Think I'll return to the hotel this evening and try to catch up on my rest." I yawned.

"Ah, the night is still young." He said smiling. "A beautiful lady as yourself should be out taking this town by storm." We both laughed then he commented on the concert and how wonderful he thought Ms. Angela Greene was. It was nearly eleven p.m.

before I exited the limo and slowly made my way inside the hotel.

"Good evening Ma'am." The desk clerk smiled. "Hope you had a wonderful time out this evening."

"I had a great time, thank you." I returned his smile and headed for the elevators, which took me to the floor of my room. As the doors opened I could not help but notice the door of the room next to mine and wonder if I would be awakened, once again, in the early morning hours by screams or some loud arguing. As I reached my door I was searching for my key in my bag and noticed that my door was slightly ajar. Fear spread through me as I tried to recall whether I had rushed out and not completely closed it or had some one been in my room during my absence? Perhaps someone was in there now. Just as I was about to turn and rush back down the hall towards the elevators, I heard a voice come from beyond the door.

Carole Lenzy Daniel (Marlowe)

"Are you going to keep me waiting here all night?"

"Angie!" I cried out loud. As I flung open the door she was propped up in my bed, topless with only the covers hiding her from the waist down. Her breast looked almost like perfectly shaped melons hanging there just ripe.

"Well are you?" She asked smiling reaching out her hand to me inviting me to join her in bed.

I closed and locked the door behind me then taking her hand sat on the bed next to her.

"Ought I keep you waiting all night?" I asked gently stroking her face while staring deep into her eyes.

She grabbed my hand with her free one then her lips were gently pressed against mine. Her kiss was soft and tender as only Angie's kisses could be. We parted and she whispered, "Oh Ella, It's been so long! I've been missing you terribly." I held her face in my hand

Carole Lenzy Daniel (Marlowe)

and kissed her lips passionately this time. As her hands worked at the zipper on my dress my fingers explored the contours of her exposed breasts. After a long tongue kiss my lips hungrily made their way past her cheek, down her neckline and on to her tender breast, kissing gently at her soft skin. She moaned in pleasure as my tongue toyed around her nipples then played gently with the very tip. My fingers were resting on her thigh at the entrance of her wet. As I sucked her entire nipple into my mouth I entered her soft pussy.

My fingers worked their way in and out of her as she squealed in pleasure while I continued to nibble at her breast. Her hungry pussy drew my fingers deeper inside until she came with tremendous force, while breathing heavily. I looked down into her eyes as she pulled my face close enough for our lips to interlock for another very tender kiss. She rubbed her wet against my thigh and began working her fingers between my panties and found that I was soaked with desire as she entered. She touched me gently then slid her face down to my navel.

"I want to taste you Ella." She whispered, softly kissing my navel.

Her tongue ran circles around my stomach then down between my legs. Before I could catch my breath, it was inside me slithering in and out like a serpent. I moved my hips to be able to enjoy more of this intruder, weaving its way in and out bringing me nearer to my explosion of love. I moaned softly with sheer pleasure as her tongue heightened my passion to its very end. As my juices flowed, I could feel Angie licking and tasting until the last drop was gone. I fell exhausted beside her as she crawled back up to rest her head on the pillow next to me. We lay quietly for a moment then our eyes met and we smiled at each other. I lay on my back and pulled her head to rest it on my shoulder. She softened her body next to mine and we could feel each others wet against our skin.

"What a wonderful surprise!" I said, breaking the silence.

"Did you enjoy it?"

"Very much! I had all but given up on being with you at all here in London." I rested my chin on her head.

"You should have known that I would see you." She raised her head to look into my eyes. "Ella, you're all I think about every day. When we are not together, I'm thinking about the next time we will be. Why else do you think I would have wanted you here with me in London?"

"For moral support?"

We both burst out with laughter, then she leaned on one arm, kissed my nipple and said, I lost your love once, I'll never lose it again."

"I'll never let you lose my love ever again." I moaned. "Nor will I ever lose yours."

We lay quiet again. The warmth of our bodies seemed to melt tenderly together. As I was about to doze off, I

287

Carole Lenzy Daniel (Marlowe)
thought of how Angie managed to get away and could not help but inquire.

"Just how did you manage to get away from your shadow of a manager anyway?"

"Todd? Oh, he has a meeting."

"At night?"

"Actually, early tomorrow morning, but he decided to spend the night in the hotel where the meeting will take place. I think we will be going on tour after the concerts here." She replied sleepily.

I sat up in bed to look down at her.

'Does he have any idea about us?"

She opened one eye. "Why Ella! Would it really matter if he did?"

"Of course it would matter! I already feel that he looks at me like I'm some snake in the grass just waiting to run off with his bride to be."

"He does not."

"Yes he does. Also he's been doing a very good job of keeping you away from me at those after parties. I think he is jealous of our friendship."

"You could be correct in assuming that. Todd is a very jealous person and sometimes controlling." She looked up at me. "He has somewhat of a temper too. He frightens me sometimes."

"Then why do you put up with him? You're the star."

"Yes, I know but he is the one that made it so. I feel somewhat indebted to him. There have been times when I have actually sought a new manager then changed my mind. He is an excellent promoter and manages everything very well. He keeps me working."

"But, Angie, this is so unlike you. You would never have allowed some brut to control your every move like that before. Remember, you were the one who once divorced because of wanting her own identity and space."

"Ella, it's really not like that. It's a little harder to explain than just his being somewhat aggressive."

"So, that's why you're thinking of marrying this jerk?"

Carole Lenzy Daniel (Marlowe)

"Not at all. Listen, I did not come here to explain my life." She sat up with a sigh. "I came to spend some time with you, the woman of my dreams. The one person on earth that I can truly say I do love." She kissed my lips tenderly.

"Just when will we be able to discuss your life?" I asked as our lips parted. "I'm merely inquiring because I care so much for you, Angie."

"Not tonight." She kissed me once more and placed her hand on my thigh. I began kissing her back as I felt her tongue creeping deeper down my throat. Her fingers entered my already wet vagina as I touched her back in all of the places I knew would make her come. We made passionate love, tasting each other and licking our juices. We took turns riding each other while smiling and enjoying what we were sharing to the fullest. We spoke only of our love for one another as we each climbed to reach our climaxes. We both cried out in pleasure as we did and sometime after that we must have fallen asleep.

* * *

When I awoke the next morning, Angie was gone. There was a note on the table beside the bed, which read:

Good morning gorgeous,

Hope you enjoyed last night as much as I did. Just want to let you know that I rushed to get to my room before Todd returned from his meeting. I really hope to be able to spend some time with you again before the end of the week.

As you know, you will be returning to New York then and I may very well go on tour. Tomorrow night will be our final concert here. Hope we can speak soon.

Love,

Angie

I read and re-read the note then glanced over at the clock. It was 11 a.m. and I could not believe that I had slept so late into the morning.

I spent the entire next afternoon downtown walking by shops and

Carole Lenzy Daniel (Marlowe)

coffeehouses. It was after 5 p.m. before I decided to retire to my room and rest up before the concert later. This would be the final concert performed in London. I had enjoyed myself in spite of not wanting to come. My time spent with Angie had been tender and loving as ever. I was absolutely sure that I could not live without her. I hated the thought of she and Todd together and wondered why she felt that a relationship with him was necessary.

"After all, hadn't she told me that I was the only person she knew she was in love with?" I asked myself. "Why then give up true love for the sake of a career when she's not happy?" I threw up my hands in an I give up manner and decided to nap before dressing for the evening activities.

* * *

The concert hall had been sold out and more crowded than any of the previous nights. The stage had been changed and lit with a multitude of

297

colors swirling as if blown by a gentle breeze. The musicians played gently as the crowd continued to pour in through the entrances. After an hour or so the chatter was suddenly hushed by the announcer's deep voice penetrating through its thickness.

"Ladies and Gentlemen, for one final evening of a week of absolute brilliant entertainment, I bring you the lady of the hour, The one... The only... New voice in Piano, Ms. Angela Greene!"

The hall exploded with cheers, applause and whistles as Angie entered the stage. The colored lights surrounded her as if she were a Queen gracefully curtseying before taking her Throne. After seating herself, the crowd silenced before she began playing her first melody. Her fingers graced the keys beautifully and in perfect rhythm. As I closed my eyes and listened to each note being played, I had vivid thoughts of the night we had previously spent together. How soft she felt next to me as we touched each other in warm places.

I thought of how she told me she loved me, and only me. Also, as she played that tune, I thought of how passionate our kisses had been. I had always thought of Angie as brilliant, now I knew that she must be a genius. I laid my head back to listen to every marvelous tune she played until right in the middle of one she stopped. The orchestra continued as Todd entered the stage, walked gracefully to her bench and led her by the arm into a most endearing waltz. They danced so wonderfully the crowd sighed with excitement at each and every turn. It was like watching a perfectly sculptured couple move across the stage in excellent rhythm. They gazed lovingly into each other's eyes as he took her for a final spin then released her gently and led her back to her bench. The crowd roared with cheers and whistles for a few moments until Todd exited the stage. Angie gracefully began playing where she had left off and produced a magnificent concert for the remainder of the evening.

The final after party had been even more demanding of Angie than the first. There were reporters, cameras, lights and loud chatter surrounding she and Todd the entire evening. I merely glanced and smiled at her for a quick second and nodded a "hello" in her direction before Todd turned her completely around to face towards someone he was posing for a photo. I mingled somewhat, had a few drinks and decided that I would not get to say good-bye to Angie that night, after all, and would try to see her before leaving for the Airport the next morning. It was around 1:00 a.m. when I arrived in my hotel room. Although I was tired I knew that I would not fall asleep quickly because I had napped earlier that afternoon. After preparing for bed I decided to review my plane accommodations so as to know what time to arrive at the Airport. I had a 6a.m. Flight scheduled to arrive in New York that evening.

After reviewing the contents of the ticket I put it aside and decided to watch some television for the first time since I had arrived in the hotel. I climbed into bed, propped myself up on the pillows and watched the early morning news. There was some mention of Angie's concert and how explosive it had been drawing the largest crowd ever at the concert hall. It showed different photos taken of she and Todd's waltz and some of the interviews filmed at the after party. I must have fallen asleep but was awakened by a loud crash and what seemed like shouting coming from the room next to mine. The static of the television off the air was buzzing, as I looked around dazed as to my whereabouts. I managed to find the remote to turn off the television completely. I was certain I had heard shouting coming from that same room. I got out of bed and placed my ear against the wall to try and make out what was being said.

Carole Lenzy Daniel (Marlowe)

"Get rid of it! I'll cut it out!" The man's voice shouted with a rage.

"No! You won't take it from me!" The woman's voice replied tearfully.

There was the sound of a smack and the thud of someone being beaten. I heard her quiet screams of pain as what sounded like him striking her with tremendous force. She cried out, "Please stop! I'll do anything you ask! Please don't hit me any more!"

"You fucking little cunt! Why do you make me beat you? When will you learn to do exactly as I tell you?"

I heard one final thud as if someone was being forced against the wall. There were words spoken I could not make out. Then I heard the door open and slam and what sounded like someone walking fiercely toward the elevators down the hall. I kept my ear to the wall as I could hear helpless weeping coming from the other side. I wanted to go over and comfort this woman. I picked up the receiver to call the front desk or the Police then thought the better of meddling into business that was not mine. Surely someone else must have been awakened by the loud shouting as I had. Why was nothing being done about it? I glanced over at the clock on the table and it was 4a.m. I paced for a while trying to decide if I should offer comfort to this battered soul. I suddenly remembered that I had a flight to catch in a couple of hours and had better start preparing before it got any later.

* * *

It was 5:20a.m. when I exited my room. Once inside the elevator, I could not seem to keep my eyes off the door to the room where all of the shouting and fights had occurred. As the elevator door was about to close the door to the room slowly opened. I nearly caught up my breath in horror! I could not believe my eyes. The lady exited the room and looked straight down the hall at me. She was in her robe and house slippers. She seemed to be holding her shoulder as if there was some pain. A man appeared in the doorway and seemed to indicate to her to return to the room. Before the elevator door closed completely, I read her lips. She whispered, "Ella!" The lady in the next room had been Angie all that time. I frantically pushed every button on the panel to try and open the doors before the elevator took off. It was too late.

Chapter Five

The Recall

One month had passed since I last saw Angie. That expression of pity on her face when she looked at me in the elevator still haunted me. I had gone over it again and again. All of those times I had heard that poor woman next door to me weeping, could it have really been Angie? If so, was it Todd who was the brutal beast beating her?

Carole Lenzy Daniel (Marlowe)

After all, I had not seen the man's face.

Often I would awake during the night,

thinking of the pain she must have

been in. I could still hear the thud of

the blows I imagined him inflicting

upon her. Why hadn't Angie mentioned

it? If she truly loved me as she said she

did, why would she not have trusted me

to save her from such a monster? I

would have rescued her. No matter

what it would have cost me, I would

have given anything to not have him

hurt her ever again. I wondered just

312

how long it had been going on. Also,

exactly how long had she planned on

keeping it secret.

* * *

School had started up again as mid

September brought us nearer to the fall

season. I had returned home from

London a week or so earlier than

Jessica and her family from their

summer vacation and had thought the

better of even mentioning that I had

accepted Angie's offer and traveled out

of the Country to be a guest at her

concert. The mornings had cooled somewhat and the boys were eager to get back to all of their friends at school. Jessica and Phillip had settled back into their routine of work as everything progressively returned to normal. One morning, as Jessica and I were having coffee before she left for work, she was reading the morning paper and mentioned an article she thought would be of interest to me.

"Oh Mom, you'll never guess who's getting married this weekend?" She mentioned casually.

"No, I don't suppose I could guess." I said after a sip of my coffee.

"Look here." She leaned over extending the paper out to me. "It says Angela Greene and Todd Baxter are to be married in Paris this weekend. Says the ceremony will be a private affair with only a few close acquaintances. There's more if you would like to read it. Here. I must get going before I'm late." She handed me the paper not noticing my heart racing. She rushed to put her cup in the sink and grabbed her jacket on the way to the front door.

"I'm a little surprised you weren't invited." She yelled back toward the kitchen. "After all you two have known each other for quite some time."

"Oh, I guess this is going to be one of those rush marriages." I replied trying to hide my pain. "You know how those people in show business are. They spontaneously marry on a whim and really don't have time to plan a serious wedding." I glared at the headlines above the article.

"Well, they certainly have the resources to do such things. And in Paris, how romantic it all sounds. I'm sure you and Angie will have much to talk about when you do see her again." She opened the door to head out. "You have a nice day Mom. See you after work."

"You do the same. Here, I'll lock the door behind you." She waved back and

Carole Lenzy Daniel (Marlowe)

after closing and bolting the door all I could do was lean against it and breath a deep sigh. I stood there for a long moment before going back to the table to read that article. As I sat down the headlines seemed to jump out at me as if they had been written precisely for me to read.

"Ms. Angela Greene to wed long time manager Todd Baxter in Paris."

I sat staring at the article reading and re-reading it trying to make some sense of why Angie would agree to marry this man. Was she forced? I imagined all sorts of horrible ways he could have forced her into agreeing to this wedding so soon. Especially after what had occurred in London. I took the paper with me to my room and read the article once more. As I lay back on my bed I imagined Angie being beaten by Todd at that very moment. I vowed to save her.

So what if she became his wife. What would that mean to us? We loved each other and no mere wedding would ever stop me from being with Angie whenever and wherever she wanted me to be. And she would want me to be with her just as much as I would need her to be with me. Our relationship was just beginning again, now that we had found each other. And I would be damned if I would let some jerk like Todd Baxter stop us from being together just because he called himself her husband.

* * *

Months past, Christmas had come and gone before I heard from Angie again. It was the afternoon before New Year's Eve and the snow was piled high in the yard where the boys and I were attempting to play a game of touch football. We had made a slight path that we followed to each end zone after the kick-offs. It was fun running through the snow and sometimes being tackled by the boys in their attempt to stop me from scoring a touch down. Phillip finally came to my rescue and asked if he might be able to get in the game.

"Be my guest." I said exhausted. "As a matter of fact, I do believe that I have had enough football for one afternoon."

"Come on Grandma, just one more game!" Billy shouted.

"No thanks, your father can take over from here. I'm sure he'll score more touchdowns than I ever could." I threw him a pass and headed inside. The boy's shouts and giggles showed just how much they enjoyed playing with their father. Phillip raced past each one spinning and counting down the yards as he headed for the end zone.

"Touch down!" I heard him yell as I closed the door behind me. I was wet and cold and about to shed my boots when I noticed a letter on the table next to the stairs addressed to me. After removing both boots, I picked up the letter to see just who would have been sending me mail. There was no return

Carole Lenzy Daniel (Marlowe)

address so I opened it and began

reading the contents.

   My Dearest Ella,

   I hope that you have been well. It

seems like ages since we last saw each

other. Not intended on my part. After

the London concert, we were so busy on

tour. I had hoped to return to the

States sooner but Todd had us booked

in more Countries than I was aware of.

I would love to see you New Year's Eve

Night, if you can get away. I have a

small gig to do at Raja's and would

love for you to be present so that we can

ring in the New Year together. Do you

remember our first New Year's Eve we

spent together in Chicago? It would

mean a great deal to me if you could

come. I am enclosing a ticket for you. I

hope to be able to spend some time

alone with you after the party. I have a

surprise too. Hope to see you there.

Angie

I re-read the letter then picked up

the ticket that had fallen out when I

opened the envelope. I studied it for a

moment, picked up my boots, and headed up the stairs to my room. Just as I reached the landing I heard Jessica's voice call out to me.

"Mom, did you get your letter I placed on the table next to the stairs?" She asked inquisitively.

"Yes I did. Thank you." She stood staring for a long moment and I knew her curiosity was getting the better of her.

"It's from Angie. She has invited me to a New Year's Eve party where she will be performing. She sent me a ticket." I held it out to her. Jessica quickly made her way up the stairs to read the ticket and admonish me to attend the party.

"Of course we will miss you here but how many people get offered a free night out on New Years Eve in the company of a Celebrity?

She smiled happily. "I know just the thing you should wear too. Tomorrow night, you will be Cinderella! Come on, let's get you ready for your Ball."

Before I could answer she had whisked me into my room and was throwing things out of my closet until she came up with the perfect gown.

* * *

Snow was falling again like little white balls of cotton whispering gently through the air. It was cold, but calm. I arrived at Raja's in my black Mink under which Jessica had insisted that I dress in my dark red, nearly burgundy gown off set by black and white trim and dark red shoes. I also wore the broach Angie had bought for me. As I shed my wrap at the door with the attendant's help I felt for it near my heart, to bring its luster to my attire as always. I could hear Angie's style playing at the piano before being shown to my table. As I entered the seating area my eyes were fixed on stage at Angie who seemed to be staring right through me while she played the most beautiful melody ever. I was caught up in the moment as I took my seat while she completed the

Carole Lenzy Daniel (Marlowe)
tune. The crowd roared with applause's

and cheers as our eyes met and she

smiled an approving smile. I wondered

if that smile was meant for me or for

the appreciative crowd that had come

out into the snow and cold to listen to

her ring in the New Year.

Other Artist played while the

countdown to the New Year wore on. I

sat and enjoyed the music while slowly

sipping on the free champagne that

was being offered by waiters

throughout the lounge. Some were up

dancing and the closer the countdown became the louder the musicians played. Angie played a set a half-hour before midnight. As the count reached ten minutes till the hour... then five minutes. Everyone was out of their seats shouting out the numbers at the top of their voices. I stood at one minute until the hour and when it struck midnight the crowd roared so loud I covered my ears. There were champagne tops flying everywhere. Cheers were loud and whistles filled the air. People were held together with kisses and before I knew

it I was being pulled to someone and

their lips found mine in a warm and

passionate manner. As we parted I was

surprised to see Angie standing in front

of me, smiling and looking deep into

my eyes.

"Happy New Year Ella!"

"Happy New Year." I replied stunned

by her boldness but liking it.

She squeezed my hands and held me

close to her once more.

"This place is noisy. What do you say

we get out of here?" She shouted close to

my ear.

"Let's do." I answered in a manner

for her to read my lips.

"Meet me outside at my limo. We'll go

someplace quiet, someplace familiar.

I've missed you Ella." She squeezed my

hand once again then disappeared in

the crowd.

I made my way to the exit, retrieved

my coat and was waiting at the curb

for her car. As the limo pulled around

Carole Lenzy Daniel (Marlowe)

front the driver got out to open the

door for my entrance. Angie was seated

comfortably in the opposite corner

slowly sipping champagne as she

motioned for me to sit next to her. As I

slid in close she offered me a glass,

which I took, and the ride to the hotel

seemed short and very quiet. We

occasionally glanced at each other

and smiled while sipping our

champagne. I reached for Angie's

hand and held it tight as close to my

bosom as possible. I loved her. I knew

that now and nothing would ever keep us apart again. Not even Todd Baxter.

* * *

The Car slowed to a halt as we pulled in front of the familiar hotel where we had always met in New York.

"I'll make sure the coast is clear and you come up in about ten minutes if I don't return." She smiled giving my hand a strong squeeze as she exited the limo.

"Are you sure it's safe? What about your husband?"

She gently kissed my lips and said.

"Ten minutes Ella. I'll be waiting. I love you."

With that she disappeared into the coldness of the night as I sat and wondered just how she could manage to love me and yet marry someone else. The snow had began falling quite heavily as I finished my drink and waited for the ten minutes to pass. I anticipated Angie's return and after twelve minutes or so, decided to make my way to the room that belonged to us. Our room, which we had shared so much passion in, after finding each other's love again. I could feel my body heating up and my passion flowing as I exited the elevator and knocked lightly at the door.

"Come in darling!" She whispered in that voice she always used when she felt sexy.

She was sitting up in bed with a bottle of Champagne chilling next to her.

Carole Lenzy Daniel (Marlowe)

"Happy New Year!" She said with her glass raised. "Now come and love me as never before. I do so want this night to be our night! This year to be our year! I don't know if I could live without your love Ella. Please don't ever take your love away from me, promise me you won't."

"Never!" I said as I looked down at her on the bed while I slid out of my gown. She was reaching for me and before I knew it we were locked in each other's embrace under warm covers with the fire blazing away beautifully in the fireplace. We made passionate love and after kissing slow, long warm kisses I held her next to me whispering how I loved her in her ear.

"Will you lick me?" Her face seemed as that of an innocent child when she looked up into my eyes. I kissed her forehead tenderly then motioned for her to straddle my face. Her juices were sweet and spicy as my tongue drove deeper and deeper into her womb. I gently licked all of her wetness away then fucked into her pussy hard with my rod. My tongue moved in and out of her as she rose and fell in complete ecstasy until she reached her climax. She fell limp next to me then whispered. "Your turn," through gasp of breaths.

I rolled over on top of her and all I could think of was confronting her about her marriage. As I looked into her brown eyes I knew that I needed her love more than any thing and that at that very moment none of it mattered. We were together and after all, why did I agree come here other than to taste her love and to feel her love inside me? I slowly kissed her once more then positioned my buttocks above her face and rode her tongue to a height of passion I had yet to experience. Her lovemaking was smooth and I came with much force and cries of pleasure that only Angie could bring out in me. She squeezed my buttocks tight as I shuttered with satisfaction.

"I love you Angie." I whispered after my body regained control of itself and

Carole Lenzy Daniel (Marlowe)

I lay beside her nibbling gently at her breast until falling asleep.

It must have been 2a.m. when I awoke with a need for the use of the restroom. My stammering around must have awakened Angie. She called to me as I was crawling back under the warm covers. Surprisingly, the fire was still burning in the fireplace and I snuggled close to her after kissing her tummy all the way up to her lips. She opened her eyes then turned so as not to meet mine.

"Hey, What's that all about?" I asked turning her head back toward mine.

Tears were streaming down her face as if she had been sobbing silently for some time.

"Was I that bad?" I teased.

She smiled slowly then pulling me to her she whispered, 'You've never been anything but good to me. That's why I love you so much." She turned away again. My only thought was of her that morning, in London. Standing, staring and gently whispering my name.

"Has he hurt you? If that bastard has done anything..." I began angrily.

"Oh Ella!" She sobbed. "You don't know what it's like for me. I've wanted to confide in you for some time but was afraid that you would not understand. Just how do I tell the woman I love that I've married the man who beats me and makes me do things, sometimes awful things?" She sobbed, trying to catch her breath. "I hate him, Ella! Yes, he made me what I am today and he is a wonderful manager but he has a violent   temper.   Uncontrollable

sometimes when he's using. Of course I

had to keep it out of the papers. No one

could ever find out. It would have

meant the end of my career. I had to

learn to live with it and to deal with

his rages." She paused for one moment

then in a different voice with the face

of an Angel, she said, "He rapes me too!

At first it was forcing himself into my

rooms then forcing himself on me until

I gave in. I would cry myself to sleep

sometimes afterward and did have thoughts of killing him or myself.

"No Angie!" I cried.

"Yes, there were a few band members who knew but everything was all hushed. It even reached the point where he would expect me to be ready for him after a show. That is how I was to show my gratitude. He is truly a sick man, Ella. I was so frightened of him at first. I had no one to turn to, no one to tell. He did everything imaginable to me. From sodomy to coming in my mouth and would beat me if he felt I was not gentle enough. I had to enjoy it. He made me Ella..." She began crying hysterically. I held her close to me. I felt the heat of my tears on my cheeks as I sobbed silently not wanting to show any weakness. I knew that I had to be strong for both of us. Angie trembled in my arms as she wept.

"It's all right now." I said. "I'll never let him hurt you again." I stroked her hair.

'He made me lose the baby too."

Carole Lenzy Daniel (Marlowe)

Surprisingly, I pushed her away from me so that I could look into her eyes. My face must have shown shock and disbelief.

"Yes, that's why I had to marry him. After we left London to go on tour I had to cancel a number of performances because I became very ill. After finally allowing me to consult a Doctor, It was confirmed that I was pregnant, something I had mentioned to him before departing London. Of course, fans were curious about cancelled concerts and all of the orchestra members were worried about me. This was something he could not get out of letting the public in on and he could not deny being the father. So, he decided we would be married immediately with very few guests. He said the fans would not approve of their superstar pianist, girl next door, giving birth to a bastard child. It would damage my image and eventually ruin my career.

Carole Lenzy Daniel (Marlowe)

We were married quickly. I'm sure some of the Tabloids found out and printed various issues of the event, even though every effort was made to keep them away." She sat up in the bed as if to find some comfort in her position. "I didn't know if you had heard or read anything about it." She said quietly. "I'd hoped you had not until I was able to explain. My intentions were never to hurt you in any manner." She turned to me. "I love you Ella in a way that I could never love him." She stared into space, then quietly said, "One night, after using, he accused me of being with you while we were in London. He was so high on cocaine, I thought he might overdose. After forcing himself on me he blurted out how he was aware of our relationship and that he would never allow a dike to give birth to any child of his. When I tried to deny his accusations he slapped me and called me a lying dike, lesbian. The slaps turned to hits and before I knew it I was lifted out of the bed and thrown against the wall. His speech was slurred as he called me filthy names and threatened to kill me after cutting the baby out of my stomach. I was then tossed to the floor and he began kicking me. He said he would kill you also for turning me into the lesbian he knew I was." Her hands were clasped over her mouth as she spoke and the tears ran free. "I lost the baby the next afternoon."

I stared up at her, trying to imagine the pain of those beatings. How had she managed to survive any of them? I felt the warmth of my own tears on my cheeks.

"No one knew or suspected." She sniffed. "Within a day or so I was back on stage performing as if none of it ever happened. The only difference was now I had become his wife." She sobbed quietly in my arms for a moment. I noticed some of the bruise marks and scars on her back and arms, I had supposed from his most recent violent attack. I rocked her gently as one would a newborn baby.

"You could get an annulment Angie!" I said with some ray of hope. She looked into my eyes as if with disbelief. "Look, I know your career means a great deal to you but you mean the world to me and I will not sit back and wait until this bastard finally kills you!" He could go too far during any of his cocaine rages. How could you stop him if he did?"

She stared at me and with an innocent little smile she said, "I couldn't." She climbed out of bed and started toward the bathroom. Before closing the door she called back in a calm voice, "I'm pregnant again, Ella."

* * *

I don't quite recall what happened after that. I know that I must have sat frozen in shock and disbelief for some moments before it happened. I do remember her calling from the bathroom that Todd was aware of her

Carole Lenzy Daniel (Marlowe)

new pregnancy and had forbade her to ever see me again. I remember her sobs between each word as she spoke slowly and clearly about her desperation. Then, almost in slow motion, it happened.

I was about to go to her and was half way out of the bed when the door was kicked in with a loud thud and the sound of a buzz saw filled the room. I heard a man's voice screaming and yelling above the screeching sound of the saw and could only get a glimpse of his face as he came toward me in a fit of rage, cursing and shouting obscenities. It was Todd's face all red and swollen his eyes bugged out as if he were some one else. I could hear Angie's name being mentioned somewhere in between all of the shouting. Before I could react, I felt the sting of the saw upon my thigh. I tried to move and I screamed for Angie but the saw had me penned to the bed as I watched it penetrate through my flesh and heard my bones crackle under the sharp blades as they moved slowly across my thighs, nearly at my hipbone. I remember seeing The horror on Angie's face as she was running toward me from the bathroom. She was shouting, "Todd! No! Todd! Please, for God's sake, no!"

I was nearly unconscious when I heard the smack of his fist on her flesh. I witnessed her falling and him lifting the saw from my flesh and penetrating it through her stomach in a circular motion. He continued yelling obscenities as he lifted the blood-dripping saw from her stomach and without hesitation aimed it at her head. I felt her flesh hitting me as the saw buzzed through her neck grinding flesh and cartilage, spitting it out over the walls and ceiling. I remember reaching for her and whispering a faint "Angie." With all of my strength, I tried getting out of bed but to my horror when I looked down I saw that my legs had been completely separated from my body and blood was everywhere. I felt a final jolt to the side of my head.

* * *

I regained consciousness in a hospital, a few days later. There was no one in the room, as I looked around unfamiliar as to my whereabouts. My attention was drawn to a newspaper on the table next to my bed. I tried to sit up to make out some of the words. The horror of the message brought back the pain of that night in one awful flash. It was headline news.

The Other Side of Love

"Concert Pianist, Ms. Angela Greene, murdered in lover's triangle! Jealous, enraged husband catches her in love nest with lesbian lover in Hotel room! After murdering her, turns murder weapon, a chain saw, upon himself. She was found nearly decapitated."

I turned away with a loud sigh as I felt the pain from my thighs shoot through my body. I looked down and saw bandages where my legs should have been. I rolled over and began to sob. I glanced back at the article and

Carole Lenzy Daniel (Marlowe)
saw my name. The Article also mentioned that the former Ms. Greene was three months pregnant at the time of her death. I began crying hysterically so that a team of doctors and nurses came hurrying into my room. I could hear a crowd of reporters and see flashes of lights going off outside the door as someone in uniform was blocking their entrance. I was shouting and hurling my arms uncontrollably. "Angie!" I screamed. "She can't be gone! She just can't be

gone!" I fought and shouted until the

sedation took over.

Carole Lenzy Daniel (Marlowe)

Epilogue

JFK International - New York

"Ladies and gentlemen we are experiencing a bit of turbulence as we are getting into the New York area. We ask that all passengers remain seated and in their seatbelts until the plane has landed and come to a complete stop."

The Pilot's deep voice broke into the silence of my thoughts. I glanced over at the boy who was still staring at me as I struggled to get my seatbelt fastened. I looked over at Jessica who smiled and began assisting me with the belt buckle.

"Well, that wasn't too bad of a ride but as usual, it's good to be back home." There was a jolting as the plane touched down on the landing strip. "Is everything alright Mom?"

"Everything is just fine." "Yes, I said, "from now on, everything will be just fine." I sighed. "She's at peace now back in the place where she began, Chicago.

The very place I know she would have wanted to be laid to rest." I looked up as if to search for her within the heavens and thought of the plot next to hers awaiting my arrival. We would be together in death as we were in life.

"Wherever she is I hope there is music. Lot's of gay, happy piano music that she would enjoy."

Jessica squeezed my hand in a reassuring manner.

"I'm sure there is." She said quietly.

Carole Lenzy Daniel (Marlowe)

Once again, I glanced at the boy who continued to stare. As our eyes met, I gave him a smile, which he returned with a large open grin.

"Yes," I whispered, "everything is alright now!"

About the Author

Carole Lenzy Daniel, (Marlowe), a native of Muskogee, Oklahoma resides in Stockton, California with her family. She is currently working on a new novel.

Printed in the United Kingdom
by Lightning Source UK Ltd.
99086UKS00001B/409